Teen Talks T

Teen Talks TO STOP THE YAWNS

Vicki Hatch
Marcus Sheridan

CFI
Springville, Utah

ISBN: 1-55517-818-9
e.1

Published by Cedar Fort Inc.
www.cedarfort.com

Distributed by:

Typeset by Natalie Roach
Cover design by Nicole Williams
Cover design © 2005 by Lyle Mortimer

Printed in the United States of America
10 9 8 7 6 5 4 3 2 1

Printed on acid-free paper

Contents

Teen Talks

Dedication

To my mother, who taught me to give a talk and make it interesting.

Acknowledgments

Thanks to Julie, Brian, Gary, Sarah, and Claire for letting me use the computer to write this book. Thanks especially to my husband, Scott, for his love and encouragement.

Introduction

The talks in this book come from selected topics in the *For the Strength of Youth* booklet. Talk topics are suitable for sacrament meetings, youth meetings, or other times when gospel topics are discussed.

Feel free to add to these talks as you prepare. If you are reminded of a personal experience or of something that happened to family members or friends, share the experience in your talk. Use the Topical Guide at the end of your scriptures to find additional scripture references that may apply. Always bear your testimony about the topic you are discussing. Tell how you have come to know that a particular principle is true.

Agency & Accountability

Choose ye this day, to serve the Lord God who made you.
—Moses 6:33

Heavenly Father has given all of us a great blessing: moral agency. This gift allows us to prove that we can choose between right and wrong. Every choice we make in life has a consequence. We are responsible for the choices we make, and thus we must accept the consequences that result from our choices.

President Gordon B. Hinckley said, "Have you ever looked at a great farm gate that opens and closes? If you look at the hinge, it moves ever so little. Just a little movement of that hinge creates tremendous consequences out on the perimeter. That is the way it is with our lives. It is the little decisions that make the great differences in our lives" (*Stand a Little Taller* [Salt Lake City: Deseret Book, 2001], 147).

In the Book of Mormon, Lehi taught his son Jacob about the importance of making right choices. He said, "Wherefore, men are free [to act] according to the flesh; and all things are given them which are expedient unto man. And they are free to choose liberty and eternal life, through the great Mediator of all men, or to choose captivity and death, according to the captivity and power of the devil; for he seeketh that all men might be miserable like unto himself" (2 Nephi 2:27).

Some people may feel that choosing to follow gospel principles takes away their freedom to choose. In reality, obeying God's laws increases our freedom. When we choose not to obey God's laws, the consequences of our choice may limit our future choices.

For example, suppose you're walking along a beach and you see a sign that says, "Danger—whirlpool. No swimming." You might think that the no-swimming rule restricts your choices. But you still really have many choices. You can swim somewhere else. You can walk along the beach and gather seashells. You can watch the sunset. You can go home. Or you can ignore the sign and go swimming.

If you make the last choice, you could find yourself caught in the whirlpool. Then you would not have many choices at all, especially if the current pulls you down and you drown.

So it is with spiritual choices. If we give in to temptation, we soon find ourselves caught and unable to escape. Our freedom to choose is minimized. Elder Richard G. Scott said, "Satan would convert divinely independent spirits into creatures bound by habit, restricted by appetite, and enslaved by transgression. . . . He would persuade us to improperly use the divine gift of free agency" ("The Plan for Happiness and Exaltation," *Ensign,* November 1981, 11).

The First Presidency has told us, "Right choices lead to happiness and eternal life. That is why it is so important for you to choose what is right throughout your life" (*For the Strength of Youth* [Salt Lake City: Intellectual Reserve, 2001], 4). We can decide some choices ahead of time, such as following the word of wisdom or living the law of chastity. Then, when temptations arise, we will be prepared to follow God's law. And we can remember the Old Testament scripture: "Choose you this day whom ye will serve; . . . but as for me and my house, we will serve the Lord" (Joshua 24:15).

3

Gratitude

He shall receive this blessing, if he receive it from the hand of the Lord, with a thankful heart in all things.

—D&C 62:7

Two young men were walking along a country road when they came across an old coat and a worn-out pair of shoes. In the distance, they could see the owner working in a nearby field, his back bent in the heat of the sun.

One of the boys thought it would be funny to take the man's belongings, cross the road and hide, and watch the man's reaction when he returned. The other boy thought that would not be such a good idea. As he looked at the coat and shoes, he told his companion that the man was probably poor. The boys decided to try an experiment. Instead of hiding the shoes, each boy put a silver dollar inside one of the shoes. Then they concealed themselves across the road to watch the reaction of the returning man.

Soon the man came to retrieve his belongings. He put on his coat and slid one foot into a shoe. He stopped, took his foot out of the shoe, and reached in and pulled out the silver dollar. His face revealed his astonishment. He looked around but didn't see anyone. Then he put on his other shoe. When he found the second dollar, he was greatly surprised. Overcome by his feelings, he immediately knelt on the ground to say a prayer of thanks. He spoke of his wife, who was ill, and of his children, who were hungry. He thanked the Lord for the gifts he had received from a stranger, and he asked the Lord to bless whoever had helped him.

The boys did not leave their hiding place until the man had gone. Both young men were moved by the prayer they had heard, and both felt gratitude for the experience they had shared (adapted from Bryant S. Hinckley, *Not by Bread Alone* [Salt Lake City: Bookcraft, 1955] 95).

In November 2000, President Gordon B. Hinckley gave a talk to the youth of the Church in which he listed six things they should do in their lives. These ideas have since become known as "The B's," and the first on the list is "Be Grateful."

The parable of the ten lepers in Luke 17 reminds us that although the Lord blessed all of the lepers, only one returned to give thanks. And "with a loud voice [he] glorified God" (v. 15). Like this man, we should have a spirit of gratitude in every aspect of our lives.

When we offer prayers, we thank the Lord for our blessings before asking for additional blessings. We also show the Lord our gratitude by living in accordance with his will. As we obey the commandments, serve and care for others, and live the way we should, we show the Lord how grateful we are for all that he has given us.

Education

Seek ye diligently and teach one another words of wisdom; yea, seek ye out of the best books words of wisdom; seek learning, even by study and also by faith.
—D&C 88:118

When Heber J. Grant was a young boy, he had a great desire to become a bookkeeper. He joined a bookkeeping class at Deseret University (now the University of Utah) and worked diligently to learn. Many of the students in his class noticed Heber's poor handwriting and teased him about it. They didn't mean to hurt his feelings, but Heber was sensitive to their comments. He determined that he would improve, and he resolved that one day he would become a teacher of bookkeeping and penmanship at the university.

He practiced his penmanship whenever he had spare time. After several years, he had made noticeable improvement. His writing improved so much that he was able to find a job as a bookkeeper in an insurance office, but he still wasn't satisfied. He continued to practice whenever he had a spare moment. After he began working in a bank, the bank bookkeeper gave him additional help with his penmanship. Soon Heber was earning more money before and after work—making maps and writing cards and invitations—than he earned at the bank. He even won an award for having the best penmanship in Utah.

A position eventually opened at the university for a teacher of penmanship and bookkeeping. Heber J. Grant applied and was accepted. After persistently striving to improve, he had kept his promise to himself.

Heber J. Grant often quoted Ralph Waldo Emerson, who said, "That which we persist in doing becomes easier for us to do—not that the nature of the thing is changed, but that our power to do is increased" (*Teachings of Presidents of the Church—Heber J. Grant* [Salt Lake

City: The Church of Jesus Christ of Latter-day Saints, 2002], 35).

Gaining an education requires work and persistence. President Gordon B. Hinckley said, "Be smart. Prepare. Be a good student in school. Resist thinking that what you do now doesn't matter, because it does. The pattern of study you establish during your formal schooling will in large measure affect your lifelong thirst for knowledge" (*Way to Be* [New York: Simon & Schuster, 2002], 28).

We should not only be educated academically but also spiritually. Studying the scriptures, attending seminary, and going to church will increase our ability to learn and bring us closer to the Lord. In the scriptures, he tells us to obtain a wide variety of knowledge:

"Teach ye diligently and my grace shall attend you, that you may be instructed more perfectly in theory, in principle, in doctrine, in the law of the gospel, in all things that pertain unto the kingdom of God, that are expedient for you to understand; of things both in heaven and in the earth, and under the earth; things which have been, things which are, things which must shortly come to pass; things which are at home, things which are abroad; the wars and the perplexities of the nations, and the judgments which are on the land; and a knowledge also of countries and of kingdoms—that ye may be prepared in all things" (D&C 88:78–80).

The Lord has given us the ability to learn so that we can become more like him. Through our persistence and hard work, we can educate ourselves throughout our lives.

Dress & Appearance

And they did not wear costly apparel, yet they were
neat and comely.
—Alma 1:27

Many families enjoy driving past the temple. Even young children can recognize the temple and will point it out. A reverent feeling surrounds the temple, and just walking on temple grounds allows you to feel the Spirit. How would you feel if you saw the temple covered with graffiti? How would you feel if the grounds were not beautifully landscaped and there were garbage and clutter around the temple? Our Heavenly Father might feel much the same way if we were to dress in an immodest fashion.

Paul taught the Corinthians, "Know ye not that ye are the temple of God, and that the Spirit of God dwelleth in you? . . . The temple of God is holy, which temple ye are" (1 Corinthians 3:16–17).

The way we dress reflects the way we feel about our bodies. If we recognize our bodies as sacred creations, like the temple, then we will dress in a way that shows our respect.

The *For the Strength of Youth* booklet tells us, "Immodest clothing includes short shorts and skirts, tight clothing, shirts that do not cover the stomach, and other revealing attire. Young women should wear clothing that covers the shoulder and avoid clothing that is low-cut in the front or the back or revealing in any other manner. Young men should also maintain modesty in their appearance. All should avoid extremes in clothing, appearance, and hairstyle" (*For the Strength of Youth,* 15–16).

The booklet doesn't say modesty is only for girls. It doesn't say "unless you are under age 10" or "except for really cute sleeveless dresses in the spring" or "except for your prom dress." We need to dress modestly and respectfully at all times.

Carol B. Thomas, a member of the General Young Women Presidency, read a letter from a young woman about this topic. It said:

"I am an average Mormon girl. Being able to keep my life this steady and strong has not been easy. I make goals all the time to help strengthen my testimony and my standards.

"Recently we had a Mutual activity on the importance of modesty. Every lesson before I felt like I was a modest dresser, but I knew there was still something I could change—my shorts and the length of my skirts. It was the one weakness that I knew I had but had placed far behind in my head. Everyone wore short shorts . . . and miniskirts, and I had bought mine with my own money. Then I heard the lesson on modesty. I went home wanting to go straight to my closet and throw away everything that was not modest so it wouldn't be there to tempt me. After[ward], I told my parents. I guess I was looking for them to tell me that there was no problem in the way I dressed and then let me go.

"Later that night my dad told me he was proud of me and that he would like to buy me a couple of knee-length dresses for church. The next step was to go through all my clothes and give away everything. It was hard for me to part with my favorite skirts and the shorts that I loved so much, but I did. *You will never see me in short shorts or short skirts again.*

"I have never felt better about myself. I love being

able to walk into the temple and church and feel like I am a child of God and am representing Him . . . by the clothes that I wear" (Carol B. Thomas, "Spiritual Power of Our Baptism," *Ensign,* May 1999, 93).

Entertainment

Let virtue garnish thy thoughts unceasingly; then shall thy confidence wax strong in the presence of God; and . . . the Holy Ghost shall be thy constant companion.

—D&C 121:45–46

Everything you see and hear affects you—either for good or bad. Consider the amount of time you spend each day listening to the radio or CDs, watching television, viewing videos or DVDs, using the internet, or reading books, magazines, or newspapers. Is everything you see and hear uplifting?

A great deal of good entertainment is available to us today, but a great deal of negative, offensive, and harmful entertainment is also available to us. Harmful entertainment is one of the most effective tools the adversary uses to deceive us into thinking that things that are evil are actually normal. Satan would have us believe that things which seem exciting for the moment are not going to affect us in the long run.

Modern-day prophets have counseled us not to "attend, view, or participate in entertainment that is vulgar, immoral, violent, or pornographic in any way. Do not participate in entertainment that in any way presents immorality or violent behavior as acceptable" (*For the Strength of Youth*, 17).

President Gordon B. Hinckley has spoken extensively about the importance of avoiding offensive entertainment. He compared such evil to Goliath, the giant David faced in the Old Testament. Goliath was armed with body armor and with a sword, spear, and shield. He was nine feet tall. He was certainly a formidable opponent, but David was armed with faith, and with the help of God he was able to defeat his enemy.

President Hinckley said, "Pornography [is] seductive, interesting, and inviting. It has become a great industry, producing magazines, films, and other materials. It is available on the Internet and, if you allow, it will intrude into your home via your television. It is designed to take your money and lead you toward activities that utterly destroy. . . .

"[But] victory will be yours. There is not a person in this Church who needs to succumb to any of these forces. You are a child of God. You have His power within you to sustain you. You have the right to call upon God to protect you. Do not let Goliath frighten you. Stand your ground and hold your place, and you will be triumphant" ("Overpowering the Goliaths in Our Lives," *Ensign,* January 2002, 2).

Even though entertainment is such a pervasive part of our lives, we can control what we listen to and watch. We can turn off the TV and computer, walk out of a movie, change a radio station, or put down a magazine. When we do these things, we keep our minds clean and pure. Then, with the companionship of the Spirit, we can choose uplifting entertainment instead.

Language

Let no corrupt communication proceed out of your mouth, but that which is good.
—Ephesians 4:29

President Spencer W. Kimball underwent several surgeries during his life. Following one of these operations, the hospital worker pushing the gurney stumbled and, in his frustration, took the name of the Lord in vain. President Kimball, weakened from surgery, looked at the young man and said, "Please! Please! That is my Lord whose name you revile." For a few moments, silence filled the air. Then the young man, in a softened voice, said, "I'm sorry" (Spencer W. Kimball, *The Teachings of Spencer W. Kimball,* ed. Edward L. Kimball [Salt Lake City: Bookcraft, 1982], 198).

For the Strength of Youth teaches us that when we use the names of God and Jesus Christ, we should do so with reverence and respect. Misusing their names is a sin. Additionally, the way we speak reveals much about who we are.

We influence others, and others judge us, by the way we speak. We choose what we say. We can choose to use language that uplifts others. We can decide to say things that are positive and complimentary. We can choose not to use language that is degrading or demeaning. We can choose not to use profanity. When we use appropriate language, we invite the Spirit to be with us.

In the New Testament, James taught the importance of governing the tongue. He said that using a bit in a horse's mouth allows the rider to turn the entire body of the horse. Similarly, a large ship can be turned, even in strong winds, by a small helm. James likened these things to our tongues—though the tongue is small, that which comes from it can have a great effect (James 3:2–6).

If we have a habit of using foul language, we can break that habit. We can decide to change our language. We can pray for guidance and help. Then we can practice by keeping quiet or thinking of something better to say when we are tempted to use foul language.

Repentance

Wherefore teach it unto your children, that all men,
everywhere, must repent, or they can in nowise
inherit the kingdom of God.
—Moses 6:57

A six-year-old boy was playing at the home of a friend named Tony when the two boys decided to slip into Tony's older brother's room to play. Tony's brother had a number of fish tanks holding a beautiful collection of tropical fish from several places around the world. The young boys decided that the fish might be hungry and, not knowing any better, gave them as much food as they could eat—much more than they needed. Soon the fish began to die.

The boys then began moving fish from one tank to another with their hands, dropping several of them on the floor in the process. By the time they had finished playing with the fish, at least ten had died.

Upon arriving home from work, the father of the six-year-old learned what had happened and went to speak to his son. After listening to the boy's explanation, the father asked, "What do you think we ought to do?"

After some discussion, they concluded that the boy should go to the neighbor's house, tell Tony's brother he was sorry, and make restitution. The boy had saved seven dollars, including several dollars he had received just days before for his birthday. His father suggested that he bring all of his money. The boy began to cry, telling his father he didn't want to give away his money. His father told him that he should pray about it. So the boy went to his room and shut the door. A few minutes later he came out with his seven dollars.

Together, father and son walked down the street to the neighbor's home. The older brother answered the door, and he was obviously upset. The father nudged his son, who said, "I'm sorry I killed all your fish."

The older boy said, "Well, I'm really mad and upset. Those fish were special to me. My dad gave them to me, and now they're dead."

The boy apologized again.

"Well, okay, but don't ever do it again."

"I want to pay for your fish," said the young boy, holding out his money.

"No, that won't be necessary," said the older boy. But a look from the father told him that he should take something. "Well, all right. How about if I take two dollars?"

His father suggested three dollars, to which his son replied, "I think that would be fair." Then he handed three dollars to Tony's brother.

As he and his father walked home, the young boy seemed much happier. He was thankful that he had repented. He said, "Dad, I'm glad we went down there. It was right, wasn't it?" (adapted from Gene R. Cook, *Raising Up a Family to the Lord* [Salt Lake City: Deseret Book, 1993], 173–75).

When we repent we receive forgiveness for our sins. Through the power of the Atonement, we can feel the peace of the Lord Jesus Christ. This peaceful feeling strengthens us and helps us to live better lives.

Sometimes we may think that our sins are too great and that we cannot repent. These feelings come from the adversary, who doesn't want us to repent. Satan knows that if we fail to repent, we won't enjoy the feeling of peace that makes us want to do better.

The Lord has promised that we can be forgiven if we repent. "Behold, he who has repented of his sins, the same is forgiven, and I, the Lord, remember them no more" (D&C 58:42).

Honesty

And let every man deal honestly, and be alike among this people, and receive alike, that ye may be one.

—D&C 51:9

Mohandas Gandhi once said that there were 999 people who believed in honesty for every single honest man. Small children are taught that being honest means telling the truth, but there's much more to honesty than not speaking falsehoods. Honesty is a way of living. It involves personal integrity that regulates the way we act in given situations.

Many years ago Elder Sterling W. Sill spoke of an opportunity he had to demonstrate honesty. While traveling through Arizona with his family, his children asked for a soda after the family had stopped at a gas station. Elder Sill went to the vending machine, where a bottle of soda cost ten cents. He put in a dime and got a soda. He put in another dime, and out came another bottle. But when he inserted a third dime, two bottles came out.

Elder Sill took the four sodas to the car, thinking, "Well, they charge too much for this stuff anyway." But then another thought came to his mind: "Sterling, if you're going to be a crook, you'd better get more than ten cents out of it." He then returned to the machine and inserted another dime (Sterling W. Sill, "The Convert," *New Era,* February 1973, 44).

A dime may not seem like a lot of money, hardly worth the extra effort of returning to the machine. But it doesn't matter if it is ten cents or ten thousand dollars. The issue is our personal integrity and whether we will follow the commandments "Thou shalt not steal" and "Thou shalt not bear false witness."

In the Book of Mormon, the people of Ammon

were "distinguished for their zeal towards God, and also towards men; for they were perfectly honest and upright in all things" (Alma 27:27). These people had buried their weapons and made an oath never to take up arms against another person. Their oath took courage, and their ability to be "perfectly honest and upright in all things" required a firm commitment.

For us, being honest requires the same courage and commitment. We need to be honest with others, with ourselves, and with God. We should not cheat, steal, or lie. We cannot permit ourselves to justify dishonest behavior just because other people around us are dishonest. We cannot rationalize dishonesty by saying, "Well, it's only a dime."

President Hinckley has said, "Be true to others and to yourself by telling the truth. Become known as someone who is unfailingly honest. Don't ever cheat. How would you like to have an operation on which your life depended done by a doctor who had cheated his way through medical school? It's better to fail than to cheat" (Gordon B. Hinckley, *Way to Be*, 77).

When we are honest, we strengthen our character, we enjoy the Spirit, and we have peace of mind. Being honest allows us to be of greater service to God because he knows he can trust us.

The Sabbath Day

Remember the sabbath day, to keep it holy.
—Exodus 20:8

The Sabbath day is one day each week set aside as a day to worship the Lord and to rest from our labors. The Lord himself set the example when he rested from his labors on the seventh day following the creation of the world.

We can participate in many wholesome activities on the Sabbath. We can go to church meetings, spend time with our families, study the scriptures and other gospel material, write in journals, write letters, do family history work, visit the sick, fast, pray, or listen to uplifting music. *For the Strength of Youth* tells us that our "dress before, during, and after church meetings should show respect for the Sabbath" (32).

Modern prophets have counseled against shopping on the Sabbath day. Recreation or athletic events are also not appropriate on the Lord's day. We have even been told to avoid jobs that require Sunday work, although some professions, such as medicine, necessarily require it.

When Elder Gene R. Cook was a young man, he had a paper route that he kept for five years. When he was sixteen, the newspaper manager offered him a job as assistant manager of circulation. He was to work in the office for a few hours after he had finished his afternoon paper deliveries, answering the phone and supervising other paperboys. His pay would triple.

Gene was grateful to have such a great job, especially because jobs for teenagers were hard to come by at the time. He was trying to save money for a mission, and the increase in pay would really help.

A few years later, the newspaper manager offered

Gene another position. The newspaper was going to begin Sunday morning delivery, and Gene was to deliver papers in the morning and then spend 7 A.M. to 2 P.M. in the office. He would get a 30 percent pay increase.

The manager told him, "I know you're a Mormon, . . . but if you don't take the job you'll lose your paper route and be fired from your weekday job as well." He explained how easy it would be to find another boy who would be willing to do the job. Gene said he'd get back to him with an answer in a few days.

Gene thought over the proposition. He wondered why he needed to make such a choice. He had been trying to keep the commandments. He had paid his tithing and was saving for a mission, but now he might lose his job. He asked his father and his bishop for advice. Both told him to pray about his decision. Gene knew that he could attend sacrament meeting in another ward that met later in the afternoon, but he would miss the meetings in his own ward.

A few days later, Gene told his manager, "I love my job and my route, but I cannot work on Sunday and miss all my church meetings. It's not right."

His manager yelled, "You're fired! Come in Saturday and pick up your last check. You're a very ungrateful young man!"

The remainder of the week was difficult for Gene, and he wondered if he had made the right choice. When he went to pick up his check on Saturday, the manager apologized for trying to persuade him to go against his beliefs. Then the manager said he had found another young man who was willing to work on Sunday, but he asked Gene if he would keep his weekday job. When Gene agreed, the manager told him the 30 percent raise would be included in his pay anyway (*Raising Up a Family to the Lord,* 244–46).

When we remember that the Sabbath is indeed the Lord's day, we are blessed. "For verily this is a day appointed unto you to rest from your labors, and to pay thy devotions unto the Most High" (D&C 59:10).

Tithing

And this shall be the beginning of the tithing of my people. And after that, those who have thus been tithed shall pay one-tenth of all their interest annually; and this shall be a standing law unto them forever.

—D&C 119:4

We have been commanded to pay a full and honest tithe, and we have been promised that if we will obey this commandment we will be blessed. Tithing is the financial means of building the kingdom of God here on the earth. Tithing funds are used for building temples and other buildings, supporting seminaries and institutes, providing Church materials to members, and publishing and translating scriptures. When we pay tithing, we show thankfulness for all that God has given us.

The Lord tells us to "prove" him by paying our tithing. When we do so, he will "open you the windows of heaven, and pour you out a blessing that there shall not be room enough to receive it" (3 Nephi 24:10). The blessings we receive from paying tithing may not necessarily be temporal blessings. We will not usually become wealthy, but the Lord will bless us with the necessities of life. The temporal blessings we do have may be protected, and we may find a way to organize our finances so that we have enough for something we didn't think we could afford. The Lord will keep his promise when we pay our tithing.

President Thomas S. Monson told of a couple that understood this lesson. They allowed a neighbor to use their pasture for his cattle. In return, the neighbor provided the couple with a large supply of beef. The couple lived in a student ward, and they made a point of sharing their meat with students who needed it.

After prayerful consideration, the couple decided to give some of the meat to the ward clerk, a brother named Jack. Jack and his wife, the Relief Society secretary, were the parents of eight children. The charitable couple didn't want to offend this family and wondered how best to share their meat with them. A few days later the couple nervously took the meat to the family's home. Jack and his wife were gracious but reserved. When their children heard why the visitors were there, they happily danced around the room.

A few months later, Jack bore his testimony in fast meeting. He said that he had always had a hard time paying tithing. It was difficult to make ends meet with such a large family. While serving as the ward clerk, he had seen other people paying their tithing, and he felt that he needed to do the same. He did so for a few months, but then he ran into a problem. In his work, he was paid a few months after completing each job. He determined that if he paid tithing, the family would run out of money for food before his next check arrived.

Jack and his wife talked to their children. They told them that if they paid their tithing they would run out of food, but if they saved their tithing they would have enough money to buy food until the late paycheck arrived. Jack wanted to buy food, but the children wanted to pay tithing. So Jack paid the tithing, and they all prayed. A few days later, their neighbors arrived with meat for the family. With this gift, the family had enough food to last until the check arrived (adapted from Thomas S. Monson, "Be Thou an Example," *Ensign,* November 1996, 44–45).

Paying an honest tithe in the right spirit will bring great blessings. Paying tithing willingly and gratefully shows that you love the Lord, that you have faith in him, and that you are his obedient servant.

Physical Health

*All saints who remember to keep and do these sayings
. . . shall receive health in their navel and marrow
to their bones; and shall find wisdom and great
treasures of knowledge, even hidden treasures; and
shall run and not be weary, and shall walk and not
faint.*
—D&C 89:18–20

When we accepted God's plan in our premortal life, we agreed to take upon ourselves a body. We have been commanded to care for this body, and we have been given a law, commonly called the Word of Wisdom, to help us fulfill this commandment. This law tells us that we should eat healthy foods and avoid harmful substances. In keeping with the spirit of the Word of Wisdom, we should also get plenty of sleep and exercise. The Lord promises great blessings to us if we keep the Word of Wisdom.

A woman came to her bishop, seeking a temple recommend. During the interview, the bishop asked her if she obeyed the Word of Wisdom. She answered that she occasionally had a cup of coffee. She said, "Now, bishop, you're not going to let that keep me from the temple, are you?" Her bishop answered, "Sister, surely *you* are not going to let a cup of coffee stand between you and the house of the Lord."

When we obey the commandments governing our physical health, we are blessed with a healthy body, a clean and alert mind, and strength and energy to go about our daily activities. We also enjoy the guidance of the Holy Ghost to help us make wise choices. When we fail to keep these commandments, we do not receive such blessings. "I, the Lord, am bound when ye do what I say; but when ye do not what I say, ye have no promise" (D&C 82:10).

Tobacco, alcohol, and other drugs are addictive and harmful to our bodies and minds. Abuse of these substances can lead to a loss of friends, family, and even life. Additionally, substance abuse leads to a loss of self-control and discernment. Often this type of impairment can lead to the violation of other commandments.

In the Old Testament, Daniel and his friends were tempted with rich food offered by the king, but they chose to eat the foods they knew to be healthy. "Daniel purposed in his heart that he would not defile himself with the portion of the king's meat, nor with the wine which he drank" (Daniel 1:8).

While the other servants ate the king's food, Daniel and his friends chose a simpler diet. After ten days, "their countenances appeared fairer and fatter in flesh than all the children which did eat the portion of the king's meat" and "in all matters of wisdom and understanding, that the king enquired of them, he found them ten times better than all the magicians and astrologers that were in all his realm" (Daniel 1:15, 20).

Not only did Daniel benefit physically from obeying the Lord's dietary guidelines, but he also benefited mentally and spiritually. So it is with us. If we obey we will be blessed with "wisdom and great treasures of knowledge" and "shall run and not be weary, and shall walk and not faint" (D&C 89:19–20).

Service

*When ye are in the service of your fellow beings ye
are only in the service of your God.*
—Mosiah 2:17

"No man can be a true Latter-day Saint who is unneighborly, who does not reach out to assist and help others. It is inherent in the very nature of the gospel that we do so. My brothers and sisters, we cannot live unto ourselves. The more we forget ourselves and lose ourselves in the service of others, the closer we draw to the Lord and His great work and kingdom" (Gordon B. Hinckley, *Stand a Little Taller,* [Salt Lake City: Deseret Book, 2001], 176).

Harold Glen Clark, the first president of the Provo Utah Temple, learned about the importance of service when he was a young man. His mother often took the needy into their home. When Harold was sixteen, his mother simultaneously cared for two grandfathers in the home. Harold was required to help bathe, dress and undress, and feed one of his grandfathers. This was sometimes difficult, especially when his friends were playing basketball outside.

One day Harold was eager to spend time with his friends, but he needed to help his grandpa get out of his wet pajamas. Harold was impatient and upset. Then he felt a shaking hand on his shoulder. He looked up and saw the tear-filled eyes of his grandpa. "God bless you, my boy," he said. "You will never regret doing this for me" (adapted from Janette C. Hales, "A Pattern of Righteousness," *Ensign,* May 1991, 84).

Harold was sorry that he had felt resentment for having to provide a service to this kind man. He learned that serving with a willing heart could make all the difference. Serving others is one of the best ways we can follow the teachings of the Savior. When we forget ourselves and devote time and energy to the service of another, we are blessed with an incredible happiness that can come in no other way.

One of our hymns suggests the joy we feel when we serve:

Have I done any good in the world today?
Have I helped anyone in need?
Have I cheered up the sad and made someone feel glad?
If not, I have failed indeed. . . .
Then wake up and do something more
Than dream of your mansion above.
Doing good is a pleasure, a joy beyond measure,
A blessing of duty and love.
(*Hymns,* no. 223)

We have many opportunities for service. We can serve at home, at church, at school, and in our community. When we serve we bless the lives of others, but we also grow. Our capacity to love increases, and we are less likely to give in to selfish desires.

The parable of the good Samaritan is a great example of service. The Samaritan gave of his own time and money to help another. We read, "He had compassion on him, and went to him, and bound up his wounds, pouring in oil and wine, and set him on his own beast, and brought him to an inn, and took care of him" (Luke 10:33–34).

Then the Samaritan gave money to the innkeeper to ensure further care for the unfortunate man. The Samaritan said, "Take care of him; and whatsoever thou spendest more, when I come again, I will repay thee"

(Luke 10:35). He did all of this for a stranger.

When we give service to others, we demonstrate our willingness to obey a commandment given by the Savior: "A new commandment I give unto you, that ye love one another. . . . By this shall all men know that ye are my disciples, if ye have love one to another" (John 13:34–35).

Living Gospel Standards

I will give unto you a pattern in all things, that ye
may not be deceived; for Satan is abroad in the land,
and he goeth forth deceiving the nations.
—D&C 52:14

As members of the Church, we are blessed to have the *For the Strength of Youth* booklet. This small book is designed to help us learn to live gospel standards in our everyday lives. It is only forty-four pages long, and some of those pages are pictures, yet the information contained in these pages is useful in every part of our lives. The directions given in this booklet come to us from our Heavenly Father through the First Presidency. They have promised that if we will live the standards discussed in *For the Strength of Youth,* we "will be able to do [our] life's work with greater wisdom and skill and bear trials with greater courage" (2).

When Elder Earl C. Tingey was living in Africa, he was assigned to visit the nation of Burundi, where he met with a government representative. Elder Tingey wanted to help the Saints in Burundi to achieve their desire to have missionaries available to teach the people, so he told the government official about the Church and how it could bless the people in his country. But the official said that the benefits offered by the Church were already available in Burundi, and he didn't believe bringing missionaries into the country was necessary.

Elder Tingey said a silent prayer, asking what he could say to say to change the mind of this government official. Suddenly, he thought of *For the Strength of Youth.* He pulled a copy of the booklet from his pocket and showed it to the government representative. Elder Tingey told him how the youth of the Church are taught the principles in the pamphlet. The man was amazed that young people were expected to live the standards in the booklet. He asked for some booklets to distribute in his own church.

After returning to Johannesburg, Elder Tingey sent five hundred copies of *For the Strength of Youth* to Burundi. About a month later, Burundi officially recognized the Church and allowed it to be established in the country (Earl C. Tingey, "Establishing Eternal Patterns," *Ensign,* October 2004).

The guidelines in the *For the Strength of Youth* booklet help us live our lives so that we can have the Spirit with us all the time. This will allow us to make correct choices so that we can live happy, productive lives. If we follow these guidelines when we are young, we develop good habits that can stay with us our entire lives. We will be prepared to serve, follow the direction of the Spirit, and someday make and keep covenants in the temple.

STOP THE YAWNS

DEDICATION

*To Mom and Dad. Words give no justice to the
positive influence you two have had on my life.
Thank you.*

ACKNOWLEDGMENTS

I would like to thank my good friends Ryan Aspy, Jon Smith, Talmadge Newsome, Jim Spiess, Jason Hughes, and Thomas Lyon for their help and influence in the production of this book. I must also thank my best friend and wife, Nikki, for her constant companionship and advice.

INTRODUCTION

A person's ability to grow and succeed is largely related to his ability to suffer embarrassment.
—Author unknown

I had my first public speaking experience as a tenth-grader in high school. I can remember the event as though it happened yesterday. My best friend was running for student body president, and he had asked me to read a speech for him in front of our fellow class members. Initially, upon his request, I thought little of the matter. Reading a speech that I didn't even have to write in front of a couple of hundred people didn't seem too challenging. But when the moment arrived in front of all of my peers, I learned firsthand what stage fright can do to someone.

As I stood in front of the audience, my hands shook, my knees wobbled, and the words just didn't seem to want to leave my mouth. In fact, I could barely even breathe, or maybe better stated, my body seemed to forget how to breathe. The eyes of the whole student body seemed to be on me. Luckily though, I was able to complete the one-page speech. Wiping the beads of sweat from my forehead, I let out a huge sigh of relief when the speech was finished, and I made myself a promise to never get in front of an audience again and relive such an embarrassing moment. I have eaten those words many times since I made that promise.

I was not a member of The Church of Jesus Christ of Latter-day Saints until my senior year in high school. Upon my conversion, I again had to confront my great fear of public speaking. This occurred the first time I bore my testimony in a sacrament meeting. I had an audience of only about forty, but I had no script to read. The only things I could depend on at the podium were the thoughts in my head and the feelings in my heart. I was still nervous, but the Holy Ghost helped me just enough to get through the moment. As I sat down after having shared my thoughts, a strange realization came over me: I was invigorated by what had just happened! It had actually felt pretty good.

From that day on, my life changed in many ways. Eventually I served a mission in Chile and become well known throughout the mission for my enthusiasm and dynamic talks. I was determined to grow in knowledge and skill with each opportunity to speak. At the end of two years, I wanted to continue to do as much public speaking in church as possible.

Therefore, for the next couple of years while at college, I continued to travel on Sundays as a member of the stake mission presidency and give motivational talks to various Church units throughout the stake. During this time, I was blessed to publish my first book, *Heavenly Father's Angels: The Ultimate Missionary Guide.* A few years later, in 2002, my second book, *Stop the Yawns,* went to press. I'm excited to publish a new edition of *Stop the Yawns,* which is still so needed among the youth of the Church. To put it simply, I love life! Public speaking and teaching are my passion. And more than anything else, I give all the credit to the gospel of Jesus Christ, which has made me the person I am today. I would never have become a public speaker or developed my talents had it not been for the Church.

Being a Latter-day Saint is much more than sitting down at church on Sundays and listening to a speaker. The Lord has designed his church to help us all spiritually grow together. We accomplish this by speaking to and teaching each other. This is why it is important that every Latter-day Saint become an effective speaker and teacher. If I can do it, anyone can do it. It just takes practice and knowledge. This book is meant to provide you with such knowledge, which will, in turn, enable you to maximize your speaking and teaching talents.

Even though I am the author of this book, I often review its contents to remind myself of things I can do better. You will find that as you read it, apply its principles to your talks and lessons, and continue to practice, your abilities will improve greatly. If you already don't have a love for public speaking and teaching, you will find that the application of the principles within these pages will help you enjoy sharing your thoughts with an audience. Public speaking is one of the most exhilarating and spiritually stimulating activities we can do. It is also a wonderful way to help build the kingdom of God on earth. My desire is that you open your mind to the teachings found in this book. I know they work. They are tried and tested. You now have them in your hands.

Whether you are a confident speaker or are scared to death to give a talk in sacrament meeting, this book has the potential to change your life. As you learn at a young age to express your thoughts to an audience, you will automatically be ahead of the game, gaining respect from your peers and others. This ability will have a tremendous influence on your future success—whether in school, during extracurricular activities, on sports teams, at job interviews, in the mission field, and so forth. The power of the word will be something you will use for good the rest of your life. What a blessing it is to learn these skills while you're young!

1
THE AMAZING POWER OF ENTHUSIASM

Nothing great was ever achieved without enthusiasm.
—Ralph Waldo Emerson

My findings have shown that great LDS speakers have mastered four abilities:

1. The ability to show passion and enthusiasm.

2. The ability to effectively tell stories and share personal experiences.

3. The ability to use powerful quotes and scriptures.

4. The ability to speak and act with the guidance of the Holy Spirit.

This book covers only the first three abilities. Hundreds

of other books teach us how to have the influence of the Spirit in our lives. I strongly feel that a speaker's ability to speak and act with the Spirit is more essential than any technique or skill mentioned in this book.

The majority of the Church's well-known speakers share the abilities mentioned above, including President Gordon B. Hinckley, President Thomas S. Monson, and authors John Bytheway and Stephen R. Covey. All of these men speak with passion and enthusiasm. They clearly understand the effect their enthusiasm has on listeners. By the time you finish reading this book, I hope that you will be on your way to developing this quality.

The first chapter of my last book is about enthusiasm and how the best missionaries are the ones that are the most enthusiastic. Is this a coincidence? Of course not! The more passionate and enthusiastic you are about the gospel, the more others will see your fire and have a desire to experience the same feelings in their lives. Enthusiasm has always been contagious and always will be.

The same thing applies to your social life. It doesn't matter whether you are tall or short, large or small, black or white, rich or poor, the one quality that will influence your popularity more than any other is enthusiasm. Your peers want to feel good. They want to be lifted up. Your job, as their friend, is to be enthusiastic for life and help them to feel good about themselves.

Whenever I am asked to give a talk in church, I always choose a topic that I am most passionate about and can relate to. For example, it would be hard for me to give a talk about the impact that Primary has had on my life. I wasn't baptized until I was seventeen, so I never attended Primary. On the other hand, I enjoy giving talks about missionary work. This is because I was taught by missionaries, I've been a missionary, and I love spreading the gospel. The next time you're given the opportunity to choose a topic for your next talk in sacrament meeting, choose something that gets you excited. If you do this, you will find the process of preparation and delivery a much more enjoyable experience.

Enthusiasm is your best tool to ensure that your audience stays awake. Sometimes I sit in sacrament meeting and observe how the actions of the audience directly correlate with the actions of the speaker. Usually, when the speaker is not passionate or enthusiastic, there are yawns, bobbing heads, and blank faces. Conversely, if a speaker is dynamic, uplifting, and confident, I see smiles, attentive faces, and people on the edges of their seats, focusing directly on the speaker.

Your goal as a speaker and teacher is to ensure that your audience is in some way positively affected by the things you do and say. If this weren't your goal, you wouldn't be reading this book. Here's your first key: Get happy and excited about the subjects you speak about, and you will see great results.

What do you think general conference would be like if President Hinckley stood up in front of the world and did not smile, showed no twinkle in his eye, and acted as if he didn't care about the messages that were about to be given? What kind of tone would that set for conference? One of the reasons President Hinckley has been embraced by members and nonmembers around the world is that he is a passionate man. He believes in what he says. Even after ninety-plus years of life, he stands tall and speaks to all who will listen. He is eager to tell his message—the Lord's message. Above all, he is sincere. When you watch him speak, you know that he follows his own counsel. That is what makes him great.

Throughout my travels as a speaker, I have found that not only are enthusiasm and passion critical during a talk but also before and after. For example, whenever I am about to give a talk, I try to show energy and enthusiasm as soon as I set foot in a chapel. I smile as much as possible, walk with a bounce in my step, and shake hands with every member I meet. I do this for two reasons: First, these actions fuel the energy and add to the excitement of my talk's delivery. Second, because enthusiasm is contagious, a speaker's enthusiasm helps listeners get into the proper frame of mind and become excited about what a speaker has to say. This is important because as we will see later, speakers can be stimulated by the energy and participation of their listeners.

Even after giving a talk, speakers should continue to be enthusiastic. I once heard a great talk by an enthusiastic, skilled speaker who spoke with the Spirit. The audience listened closely to what he said. After the speaker finished, I approached him, introduced myself, and excitedly told him how much I had enjoyed his powerful words. Instead of showing the same enthusiasm he had exhibited ten minutes before, he simply gave me a dull look and said something like, "Oh, well, thanks," and then went on his way. Needless to say, I was disappointed in his lack of interest, which is my lasting memory of this individual, rather than his talk.

When I say that we must have enthusiasm as speakers, I don't just mean it to be a temporary character trait. Enthusiasm needs to be a part of who we are. Everyone has the ability to show energy and excitement, whether it be for a gospel principle or for life in general. It may not come as easy for some as it does for others, but it can be developed over time. It just takes effort and practice.

Once you have mastered the ability to be enthusiastic at your speaking engagements, you will have won most of the battle. Everything else will fall into place once you have developed this trait. Let this be the top goal you set for yourself while reading this book. Be enthusiastic. Be a motivator. Lift others. Smile. Always take a positive perspective. Let your light shine forth. As you do so, you will find that the number of friends you have will grow, your confidence will soar, and your ability to speak in public will become a strength. It's that simple.

2
THE POWER OF PERSONAL EXPERIENCE

Condense some daily experience into a glowing symbol, and an audience is electrified.
—R. W. Emerson

In preparing to write this book, I asked many Church members who their favorite speaker was. More than half told me that they enjoyed listening to President Thomas S. Monson the most. I next asked these members what they found so appealing about President Monson. Their answer was usually the same—listening to President Monson's stories. I must concur. President Monson is the greatest storyteller I have ever heard. It seems that he has a story for just about every gospel topic. I would say that more than 75 percent of his talks consist of personal experiences from his life.

President Monson has mastered the technique of storytelling. He uses this skill to maximize the effectiveness of his talks, thereby making a lasting impression on his audience. In his talks, President Monson tells us what life has taught him. That is why we are so eager to listen to his words.

This chapter is meant to answer two important questions: (1) Why are personal experiences and stories such a powerful tool for speakers? (2) What skills go into telling a great story?

For your message to hold any weight with your listeners, you must get their attention (via enthusiasm) and then say something that has a lasting impact on them (a powerful story). Your message should not be something that leaves their minds as soon as you leave the pulpit.

For example, let's say you give a talk in sacrament meeting and someone comes up to you afterward and says, "I really liked your talk today." You respond, "Well, thank you for your kind words, Sister Smith. Please tell me what it was about the talk that you found most interesting." If she says, "Well, I just thought it was all good," it's likely that she is just being nice. But if Sister Smith says something like, "Well, that story you told about going to the temple—I could really relate to that," then you know that what you have said really did have an impact on Sister Smith. Such should be your goal with any talk.

It always amazes me when a person speaks to an

audience for twenty minutes and doesn't share a personal experience. This is like doing the backstroke with your hands tied behind your back.

At your next sacrament meeting, observe the difference in the congregation's focus when a speaker shares a personal experience. Heads will pop up, and those who may have been daydreaming will begin to pay attention. I have witnessed this hundreds of times. It is truly amazing what a difference a good personal experience or story can make.

Whenever I have counseled members on this matter, I have often heard the response: "I just don't have any good stories to tell, and besides, no one is interested in my life." People love to hear about the lives of others. Think of all the books, TV shows, and magazines whose sole purpose is to tell us about the lives of other people. This desire to know about others is also the root of all gossip in our society. If you have had an experience in your life that has stuck with you throughout the years, it is likely that it will be of interest to others.

We have all had interesting events occur in our lives; sometimes it just takes creativity and energy on the speaker's part to make the story an interesting one. For example, I often use the following simple story when speaking to my audiences about becoming spiritually lazy. (This story is much more effective when you see it spoken and acted out, but reading it will have to suffice for now.)

One day, not long after I had returned home from my mission, I was cutting grass with a self-propelled mower.

After having cut most of the yard, I was left with an area of grass that was about twenty feet by twenty feet. The grass in this small area had grown thick, so I had to push the handles of the lawn mower downward so that the front of the mower would come off the ground a few inches. This raised the blade, allowing me to go over the thick grass without having the lawn mower cut out on me.

As soon as I began to cut the thick section of grass, I noticed that I had gone over a baby turtle. Luckily, though, the turtle had not been touched by the lawn mower's blade. I was relieved that I had not hurt the beautiful little animal and placed it in the woods. At this point, I realized that because the grass was so thick in the area I was cutting, I would need to be careful to watch out for any other turtles.

I then proceeded to cut the grass, raising the mower blade the whole time so that no accidents would occur. After a few minutes, all that remained was a small strip of thick grass. It was only a few feet long and about four inches wide. Because the area was so small, I decided to lower the front end of the mower. I concluded that there would be little chance of the mower cutting out or running over anything.

As I made my final shove, I heard a loud snap come from under the mower. My heart started to beat faster as I turned off the mower and pushed it forward to see what I had hit. My jaw dropped as I saw another baby turtle. This time, though, it had not been so lucky. Its body was torn to shreds. Sorrow filled my heart. Because I had dropped my guard for only a few seconds, I had killed a baby turtle. As I looked at the baby turtle and pondered what I had done, I promised myself to never drop my guard again.

Then I add, "Brothers and sisters, this is how Satan works. He waits until we are in a comfort zone and feel that we do not have to beware of his temptations any longer. No matter how far we have come or what we have done, Satan will always be waiting for us to drop our guard. My challenge for you young men and young women today is to keep your guard up, and your reward will be well worth the effort spent."

As you can see, this is a simple story with a powerful message. I once related this story in a sacrament meeting. A member came up to me afterward and said, "Marc, I don't know where you get these crazy stories from, but you sure had me going!" The truth is, most people just forget about incidents that occur in their lives because they feel that they aren't important. I see it this way: If any experience that I have had has taught me a lesson in some way, then it will likely teach others as well.

Now that I've established the general need to use personal experiences or stories in our talks, let's look at eleven important keys for effective storytelling.

ELEVEN KEYS OF EFFECTIVE STORYTELLING

1. Use hand gestures and actions. A major key to the effectiveness of any story is the speaker's ability to use hand gestures and actions in such a way that it is easier for the audience to relive the experience with the speaker. No matter how interesting or exciting a story may be, if speakers don't bother to move an inch and if they look as if their arms are tied to the podium, the audience will be less engaged. For example, I often share an experience I had one day when I looked out of my apartment and saw two elders in the freezing cold and snow laughing and smiling while they slid down a parking lot. When describing this incident to an audience, I always demonstrate the way the elders laughed at each other and what they looked liked as they slid in the snow. This bit of theatrics has always proven effective because I know that when I do this, even the youngest children in the congregation stop their playing and coloring and take a peek to see what I'm doing. I'm not advocating that you should be doing jumping jacks while giving a talk, however. Everything must be done in moderation and in accordance with what the Spirit indicates.

2. Use names of characters. This is an important aspect of storytelling that many speakers often overlook. Using names helps listeners to follow the speaker and adds feeling to what the speaker is saying. Take note the next time President Monson gives a talk. When he tells his stories, he always mentions the names of the characters.

3. Don't let your stories carry on too long. I have made this mistake many times, as have most speakers. No matter how good you think your story is, keep it brief. This way, you won't lose your audience, and they'll be tuned in to most of what you have to say. I recommend that you keep any story under five minutes.

4. Tell stories that your audience can understand. This is a critical aspect of any talk. You must talk at the level of your audience and relate to them with any stories you tell. For example, I gave a youth fireside talk shortly after I had returned home from my mission to about seventy-five young people. I prepared well for the talk and thought that it would do well, but I made the mistake of mostly telling missionary experiences. The talk turned out to be pretty much a dud. I could tell from the audience's reaction while I spoke that they weren't greatly interested in what I was saying. Who can blame them? They were listening to stories that they could not yet relate to. I learned a lot from this experience and haven't made the same mistake since. We will talk more in chapter four about how to relate to an audience.

5. Avoid reading stories from a book. I have seen many speakers in sacrament meeting read stories from the *Ensign* or from books by LDS authors. Although these stories are often good, it is usually better that the speaker read and become familiar with the story beforehand. By doing this, the speaker can then recount the story, thus making more eye contact with the audience and showing more emotion and enthusiasm. These actions will help the audience remain alert and interested in what is being said.

6. Make your point at the end of each story. Just as I did with my turtle story, so you should end each story you share by making a point. This is because most stories resolve at the end, which draws the interest level of the audience to a peak. A speaker must take advantage of these moments and say something that the audience will internalize. This is also a good time to challenge the audience and admonish them to follow a certain gospel principle.

7. Do not share past transgressions. The Spirit is a sensitive thing. It comes and goes easily. One way to make it leave quickly is to relate past transgressions. They are usually an unnecessary element of any talk. Admitting that you are imperfect is fine, but keep the details to a minimum.

8. Fluctuate your tone. This one goes with making hand gestures. All of the best orators I have ever listened to are masters at varying their voices in order to make the maximum impact on their audience. John Bytheway is skilled at this. Listening to John is like riding on a spiritual and emotional roller coaster. This quality helps make him the most sought-after youth speaker in our church today.

9. Be descriptive. Details are important because they spark the imagination of your listeners. Whenever you tell a story, you want everyone in the audience to picture in your mind what you are saying. Details make this picture much clearer.

10. Get excited! We have already talked a lot about enthusiasm, but we must again take note of its importance. Before you begin to relate an experience, let your audience know that you are excited to share with them the message you have prepared. Also, it's effective to let them know that what you are about to say is interesting and that they will be affected in some way. For example:

"Brothers and sisters, I am excited to share with you a personal experience that has changed my life. I think you'll find it very interesting . . ." As you can see, it only takes a few sentences to make this important point. Giving an introduction in this manner will draw the attention of the audience and help you build up to the climax and message of the story.

11. Practice telling your stories beforehand. If you practice telling your stories before you actually give a talk, you will be able to work out the kinks as well as work on the previous ten keys. You can do this by telling your story to friends, a spouse, or even the mirror. I have often told my wife stories before sharing them in a talk or conference. On numerous occasions she has helped me correct simple mistakes that would have detracted from the effectiveness of the stories.

3
USING SCRIPTURES AND QUOTES EFFECTIVELY

And the Book of Mormon and the holy scriptures are given of me for your instruction; and the power of my Spirit quickeneth all things.
—D&C 33:16

Next to being witty yourself, the best thing is being able to quote another's wit.
—Christian Nevell Bovee

How would you feel if you were given the opportunity to have the Savior himself participate in your next talk or lesson? What would you say if Alma offered to be a guest speaker at a fireside about missionary work? Better yet, how would you feel if Joseph Smith were willing to share a few words at your next Gospel Doctrine class? All of these scenarios are still possible in our church today. We have the means of using these wonderful servants of the Lord whenever we need them. How? By turning to the standard works, of course! They're always within arm's reach.

What a wonderful tool the scriptures are. Although scriptures and quotes usually take up little of the actual time we spend in front of an audience, they can have a monumental impact on the direction and overall effectiveness of a talk. We'll discuss why we use quotes and scriptures in this chapter and also the ways in which we can use them more effectively.

The words of the Lord and his servants are important to us. They lead and guide us, and they affect each of us in different ways. They teach, inspire, guide, and motivate. Their beauty and influence are endless. We must we take advantage of them. After all, scripture is the Lord's word. He is the best teacher of all. If you, as a speaker, can bring the scriptures to life for your audiences, you can affect them in a positive and profound way. This may be difficult, but with enthusiasm and help from the Holy Ghost, it can happen. I have listed five keys to effective use of scriptures and quotes in talks:

FIVE KEYS TO USING SCRIPTURES AND QUOTES

1. Share scripture background. I have heard

countless speakers share scriptures without telling their audiences anything about the history or background of the text. This can damage to the impact of what the scripture is saying. For example, let's say you are teaching a group of new members a lesson on obedience. You would like to use 1 Nephi 3:7 to make your point. Do you (1) have a class member read the scripture and then have the class comment on it? Or do you (2) discuss briefly the events that led up to 1 Nephi 3:7 and then read it?

In scenario two, you would mention the fact that when Nephi made this statement, he had already left Jerusalem, walked many miles, listened to the murmurings of his brothers, and faced much suffering in order to flee into the wilderness with his father—just to be told to return to Jerusalem to obtain the plates of brass. After explaining to your class members the scripture's context, you would then tell them to contemplate how the verse applies to us today. Finally, you have a class member read 1 Nephi 3:7 and then ask class members how the verse relates to their lives.

Can you see the difference in the two scenarios? In the first one, nothing is done to help the class understand what is happening. With this method, little thought is required, which leads to uninterested listeners and a lack of learning.

In the second scenario, Nephi's background is well-described, and class members can therefore imagine what it would have been like to be Nephi, hear his father's desires, and then follow his command. With such knowledge, 1 Nephi 3:7 will undoubtedly have more of an impact on the class. The idea of explaining the background of a scripture is nothing new, but it is often overlooked by most members, including myself. This practice can be used effectively in both lessons and talks.

2. Keep your focus on only a few scriptures. The next time you're listening to general conference, count how many scriptural references the speakers use in their talks. You'll find that most speakers use two to three scriptures per talk. This is because the more you read scriptures during a talk, the more likely your audience will tend to drift off and lose interest in what you are saying. If you focus on just a few scriptures, you will be able to spend more time conversing with your audience, which is really what they want. We should not use scriptures to fill time. We should use them to give a talk direction, balance, and spiritual insight. A speaker's personal experiences, stories, and thoughts are what should make up the majority of a talk. It is often effective and necessary to use more scriptures when teaching lessons, however, depending on the allotted time of the lesson and the subject being taught.

3. Add emotion. Can you imagine Nephi, who was "large in stature," saying in a sheepish voice, "I will go and do the things which the Lord hath commanded"? Of course not! The reading of scriptures often requires a little bit of theatrics and imagination.

For example, if you were to read 1 Nephi 3:7 in a talk, you would want to use a strong voice as well as your hands and arms to show emotion, trying to act as Nephi would have acted in that moment. By doing this, the verse will have more impact on the audience. Also, their ability to imagine what Nephi was doing and saying will be greatly enhanced. The scriptures were not meant to be read in a sheepish or monotone voice. They were meant to be spoken with power and authority.

4. Take your time and use pauses when necessary. The next time you read a scripture or quote in a talk or lesson, read the words slowly. This will give your listeners time to digest what you are saying. The same idea applies at the end of the scripture. After reading the passage, pause a few seconds. You will notice that many members of your audience will have a look of thoughtfulness on their faces. This is exactly what you want. Also, if you feel it is necessary to stress a scripture or quote to your listeners, repeat the passage. Doing this will give your audience more of a chance to contemplate the message you are trying to get across.

5. Do not overload a talk with quotes. I really enjoy a great quote. A quote is a tool we use as speakers and teachers to arouse the interest of our listeners. Quotes can be effective, humorous, and thought-provoking. In fact, Church leaders often use quotes by C. S. Lewis. Despite the potential effectiveness of quotes, they should not be used too often.

I once gave a talk that consisted of seven of my favorite quotes. I was excited to read and expound on them with my audience, but by the time I shared three of the quotes, my audience began to lose interest. By the seventh quote, I noticed many wandering eyes and blank faces. This incident taught me a great lesson. The old adage "Too much of anything can be harmful" comes to mind when I think back on this experience.

By combining the companionship of the Holy Ghost, enthusiasm, storytelling, scriptures, and quotes in your talks and lessons, you will be using the greatest tools we have been given to uplift and inspire our fellowmen.

4
THE AUDIENCE-SPEAKER RELATIONSHIP

You may use different sorts of sentences and illustrations before different sorts of audiences, but you don't—if you are wise—talk down to any audience.
—Norman Thomas

In the previous chapters, we talked about the characteristics of great talks: enthusiasm, powerful storytelling, and the effective use of scriptures and quotes. Before we move on and analyze talk preparation and delivery, we must focus on one other major aspect of any talk or lesson: the relationship you have with your audience.

No talk is a good talk without the help of a lively and participating audience. "What is a lively and participating audience?" you may ask. It is one that focuses on the speaker and that is alert and excited to know what will be said next. A participating audience is one that is more worried about hearing the message of the speaker than about looking at the long hand on the clock.

Many speakers often forget that audience participation is crucial, and they end up falling short in their efforts to have an impact on their listeners. This chapter consists of keys that will help you to better understand, as well as to maximize, your future audience-speaker relationships.

As we have already established, you are reading this book so you can become the best speaker you can be. With such a desire, you will want to do everything possible to positively affect your audience. To accomplish this, you will have to use many techniques that will enhance the relationship you have with them during a talk. As I have studied audiences and speakers, I have found that there are basically two types of audience-speaker relationships. I have dubbed them the "Happily Married" and the "Not-so-Happily-Married" relationships.

Giving a talk to an audience is similar to marriage because you are going to be with each other for an allotted time, whether you both like it or not. This can be a happy time or a difficult time, depending on what you and your audience do. But as the speaker, you set the course and tone of this relationship. It is your job to keep the other entity happy, excited, and interested in what you have to say. The best speakers and teachers will always find ways to light a fire in their audiences. The great thing about this relationship is that you can feed off the energy of your audience. Their actions and responses to your words can quicken your thoughts and enhance your abilities. At the same time, your actions as a speaker will determine the interest level and overall awareness of your audience. Simply put, when you are together, you are better. So let's talk about this marriage and all that we can do as speakers to ensure that it is a healthy and prosperous relationship.

TEN KEYS TO A HEALTHY AUDIENCE-SPEAKER RELATIONSHIP

1. Speak at the level of your audience. Few things are worse than listening to a speaker who uses words and phrases that are beyond the level of an audience. This happens often, mainly because some speakers feel that big words invite more interest from an audience. They also feel that big words make them look impressive. This is a myth. A great way to lose the interest of your audience is to use words and phrases that are beyond their comprehension. As speakers, we should never try to impress others with our abilities.

2. Select topics your audience can relate to. Can you imagine giving a talk to a youth group about the importance of starting a retirement plan? Such a talk would be almost impossible. As a speaker, you must talk about subjects that your audience can relate to. If you don't, your marriage will quickly be on the rocks. That's why you must do your best to address their interests and concerns—not just yours.

3. Learn to drop names. It is an excellent idea to utilize the names of your listeners in your talk. When an audience knows that one or more of them is actually involved in your remarks, they perk right up and wait to see what else the speaker will mention about them. People love to hear positive things about themselves. This is a surefire way to connect with your audience.

4. Learn about your audience. As with dropping names, this works great in cases where you have been asked to speak at a ward or branch to which you don't belong and know few, if any, of the members. If you want to get the interest of your audience, say something about them that they had no idea you knew. This will be sure to fascinate them and increase their willingness to listen intently to your message.

5. Show your appreciation. The act of appreciation goes a long way in life, especially in an audience-speaker relationship. Show appreciation for your audience's kind acts, and they will be more inclined to take your words to heart. Openly criticize them, and you might as well take a seat.

6. Identify with your audience. If you would like to quickly gain the support of your audience, tell them about something you both have in common. This simple act will raise their interest and lead to better audience participation.

7. Make your audience a partner in your talk. This technique is most commonly used in teaching lessons, although it can be used in talks as well. Asking questions, taking polls, and asking audience members to come forward to participate in a demonstration are just a few ways you can form a partnership with your audience.

8. Show a sense of humor. One of the few universal expressions that all people show is the smile. There is nothing compared to the knowledge that something you have said has made another person smile, laugh, or feel good inside. A great way to accomplish this is to show a sense of humor. Don't be afraid to make others laugh. Also, don't be afraid to laugh when you are speaking. This simple act will show others that you are a fun person to be around. It is also important to note, though, that not all talks and lessons are meant to be funny. Depending on the subject matter and what the Spirit indicates, you must determine when to be funny and when to be seriousness.

9. Play yourself down. A great way to lose your audience is to act as if you are better than they are. For example, let's say you're going to give a talk on tithing. It is not a good idea to start your talk by saying, "I have chosen to talk on tithing today because I have paid my tithing in exactness every month of my life, and there's no reason you all can't do the same."

Such a statement indicates that you think you're more righteous than your audience. King Benjamin is a great example of playing ourselves down. In his final major discourse to the people of Zarahemla, he states, "I have not commanded you to come up hither that ye should fear me, or that ye should think that I of myself am more than a mortal man. But I am like as yourselves" (Mosiah 2:10–11).

King Benjamin had a clear understanding of how to

relate to his audience and play himself down. Let's all follow his example.

10. Love your audience. Love is a great motivator. This is why we can feel the love our prophets have for us whenever we read or listen to their counsel. If you sincerely love your audience, your message will be more powerful, and the hearts of your listeners will open more easily.

These keys are important. Apply them to your talks and lessons, and you will see incredible results with your audiences each time you are blessed to expound on the gospel of Jesus Christ.

5
TALK PREPARATION

Spectacular achievement is always preceded by
spectacular preparation.
—Robert Schuller

Okay, you've been asked to give a talk. Great! Don't feel so gloomy. This will be a wonderful opportunity for you to learn, grow, and progress spiritually. Also, it should be a fun and enjoyable experience. Remember that when you're preparing your message. This chapter focuses on how to prepare for a talk, the steps that are involved, and several ideas that will make the process a more pleasurable and easy experience.

In our church, there are basically two types of talks. I have dubbed them the "assigned" talk and the "just speak on whatever you would like" talk. If you ever have the option of choosing your own topic, take it! This will enable you to speak on a subject that you are passionate about. It will also give you an opportunity to speak on something you know about.

If you have an opportunity to speak on a subject of your choice, ask yourself what you would most like to talk about, and then ask the Lord what he feels his sheep need to be taught. If you have already decided on a topic, confer with the Lord before proceeding. Doing this will give you more confidence and inspiration for your talk. Once you have chosen or been given a topic to speak on, your next step is to form an outline for your talk. You will use this outline as a guide and map for sharing your message. For many people, the process of forming a talk outline is a difficult one, but it doesn't need to be. The following six steps are meant to be easy, efficient, and practical for any speaker.

SIX STEPS TO FORMING A TALK OUTLINE

1. After choosing or being assigned a topic, think of experiences that you and others have had with this topic. These experiences are important and will make up the body of your talk, so reflect on your life as well as on the lives of others. If no experiences come to mind, research the Church magazines, especially the *Ensign*. The gospel library, located at www.lds.org (the Church's website) is also a great resource. This site is full of helpful information on just about any gospel topic imaginable. As you think back to experiences you have had, and as you research the words of others, write down anything that you feel could be pertinent to your talk.

2. Select two to four of these experiences or stories that could have the most impact on your audience. If you are not sure which stories to choose from, just choose your favorites. Which experiences have affected you the most? If the stories are interesting and pertinent to you, they should have that same effect on others.

3. Uncover the lessons behind the stories. Once you have selected the experiences or stories that you would like to share, discover the lessons you learned from these events. Again, record your thoughts on paper.

4. Focus on the talk's objective. Now that you have thought of the lessons learned from these experiences, understand that these lessons form to make the goal, or objective, of your talk. For example, if you learned from certain experiences that it is always a good idea to listen to the promptings of the Spirit, the objective of your talk could be to help others to listen to and obey the promptings of the Holy Spirit. Of course, with each story you have chosen, there can be a variety of lessons learned. Just remember, every story and every scripture you read should support the overall objective of the talk.

5. Find the right scriptures and quotes. Now that you have established the basic body and goal of your talk, research scriptures and quotes that will support and add meaning to your admonitions. A good idea is to use one scripture or quote with every story. That way the audience will hear evidence from three different sources—the story, the scripture or quote, and the speaker.

6. Write the outline. Now that you have the basics

(stories and scriptures), all you need to do is put these ideas down on paper by writing out a talk outline. I have listed one of my talk outlines to give you an idea of what these six steps should look like.

Sample Talk Outline

- Subject: Missionary Work
- Talk objective: Help members get excited about missionary work and desire to apply the principles taught in their own lives.
- Introduction: My love for missionary work, my conversion story.
- Lesson no. 1: Attitude and enthusiasm are important.
- Scripture no. 1: "Therefore, dearly beloved brethren, let us cheerfully do all things that lie in our power" (D&C 123:17).
- Story no. 1: How my attitude affected the success I had as a missionary.
- Lesson no. 2: The Lord will help us in times of need when we attempt to share the gospel.
- Scripture no. 2: "Open your mouths and they shall be filled, and you shall become even as Nephi of old" (D&C 33:8).
- Story no. 2: How my companion and I overcame the problem of an empty baptismal font to have a spiritual baptismal service.
- Lesson no. 3: Chosen and prepared people live everywhere. There is no such thing as a "dead" area.
- Story no. 3: The success my companion and I had in

an area that was supposedly tracted out.

- Quote: "There is no such thing as good or bad, but thinking makes it so" (Shakespeare).

CLOSING AND TESTIMONY

What I have listed is what I bring to the podium whenever I give a talk. I don't write much down on paper because all I need is an outline that will keep me on track. Too many papers and books can cause clutter and confusion. This is also why I write out the scriptures or quotes that I'm going read. Using this method makes the majority of the talk a conversation between the audience and me—hence, the word *talk.* This method is relaxing for a speaker. With its flexibility, you can use creativity as well as any promptings from the Spirit that you may feel during the course of your message.

Once you have finished an outline, practice telling your stories—whether they be from your own life or from the *Ensign.* You need to become familiar with telling your stories out loud. This is best done by practicing with a friend or relative or by simply talking to the mirror. When you practice telling your stories, be sure to use details and gestures, as mentioned earlier. Always ask your listeners for feedback, and look for ways of making your stories more clear, concise, and powerful. By doing this, you will feel more confident and comfortable when you give your talk.

Practicing your stories will also give you a good idea of the length of your talk. If you notice that your stories and thoughts carry on too long, this is your opportunity to make adjustments. Stay within your allotted time. It is inconsiderate to take time from another speaker—regardless of how grateful that speaker may be!

The principle of practice and repetition also applies to scriptures and quotes you have selected. Read over these words of counsel many times. Ponder and pray about what they are saying, and you will likely receive additional inspiration as to what to say in your talk.

One last word of advice: Don't memorize a script. Most speakers don't memorize their talks. What's wrong with memorizing a talk? First of all, it is an extremely difficult and time-consuming task. Second, most people end up having to read from their scripts because they get flustered in front of an audience and lose their place. Third, memorized talks are usually mechanical, lacking in emotion and enthusiasm. And finally, people want to hear words that come from your heart, not from the storage banks of your brain. This is also why it is usually less effective to write your entire talk on paper. By doing this, you greatly lessen your ability to speak from the heart, follow any promptings of the Spirit that you may feel during the talk, or grab the attention of your audience.

I have kept this chapter short for one main reason: As I said earlier, the preparation that a speaker puts into any talk should be an enjoyable and uplifting experience, not a grueling and mind-boggling journey. If you will stick to the advice in this chapter, you will find that the six steps mentioned here work. I have received E-mails from many Church members across the country who have used this method with great results. By following these steps and writing an outline, you will have all that you need for a successful talk.

You may have noticed that I have not discussed actual preparation time for a talk. This is because there isn't a set time for talk preparation. Some of my best talks have been prepared in twenty minutes. For other talks, I've prepared for days, only to fall on my face. As long as the talk outline is well done and has been diligently practiced, the message will most likely be effective, no matter how long the preparation time.

6
THE TALK

> *The way to develop self-confidence is to do the thing you fear and get a record of successful experiences behind you. Destiny is not a matter of chance, it is a matter of choice; it is not a thing to be waited for, it is a thing to be achieved.*
> —William Jennings Bryant

After you have done all you need to do to prepare your talk, the day arrives when you must present your thoughts to an audience. This can be a great experience or a forgettable experience. Everyone has good and bad talks. Many factors contribute to the overall effectiveness of a talk, and this chapter is meant to help you understand more in depth the factors that will make your talks consistently great.

CONTROLLING YOUR FEARS AND NERVOUSNESS

I cannot remember the last time I gave a talk and was not nervous. Nervousness is a fact of life for any speaker. All the way from President Gordon B. Hinckley to Joe Primary, Church members experience some type of nervousness when they have to give a talk. In fact, public speaking has always been one of our society's greatest fears. However, people who overcome this fear greatly improve their self-confidence and sense of well-being.

Each time we learn to conquer our fears, we are actually conquering other foes that we eventually will have to fight. Having the opportunity to overcome and grow is one of the greatest blessings offered to us by Lord's church. He wants us to develop and improve our talents. Giving talks in sacrament meeting or teaching a lesson does this. As I mentioned in the introduction, I have a strong testimony that we can develop our talents as we actively participate in the gospel of Jesus Christ. What a blessing!

We must also understand that stage fright and nervousness can actually be useful to a speaker. For example, I recently gave a sacrament meeting talk and was pretty nervous before sharing my message. My heart was beating fast, and I found myself breathing a little harder. Did this bother me? Of course not, mainly because I understood that as my heart beat faster, I could more easily show enthusiasm and be spiritually inspired. Remember this the next time you experience nervousness before you have to give a talk. Use nervousness to your advantage, and you will be surprised by the great results.

When it comes down to it, stage fright is just a natural part of the speaking process. No matter how seasoned a speaker you are, you're going to be nervous. If you are a novice speaker, take this advice to heart and plow through your fears. Each time you experience success, your enjoyment for speaking will grow. Instead of experiencing agony, the thought of sharing your thoughts and experiences will become a pleasant and pleasurable experience. In fact, the day I stop being nervous is the day I stop speaking. I know that if I have no sense of anxiety, my talks will be lifeless.

Give Yourself a Pep Talk

In the days, hours, or minutes before a speaker gives a talk, it is common to have some type of apprehension. "Am I prepared enough to share this message?" "Is this the right topic for my audience?" "What if my thoughts become jumbled and I sound silly?" "How can I get up in front of all these people?"

These are just a few of the possible questions that can run through your mind. At such times, you must combat these thoughts with a good pep talk. In clear and concise terms, tell yourself that the talk you are going to give will be great because it is derived from your own thoughts and experiences. No one else can share these experiences the way you can, so you have chosen the perfect talk for you. That is what matters most. The power of autosuggestion is one of our greatest tools to combat fear and reach new heights of greatness.

Take a Deep Breath

A classic result of nervousness is distorted breathing. Take it from me when I tell you that trying to give a speech without breathing is difficult. To understand what I am saying, the next time you read your scriptures, see if you can make it through an entire page on just one breath. You can't, which is why it's important to breathe deeply before giving a talk and while giving talk. In fact, take about a minute just before you give your next talk and focus on taking long, deep breaths. This relaxes the body, stimulates blood flow, and reduces nervousness.

THE INTRODUCTION

Finally, we get to address the actual talk, starting with the introduction. Although the introduction does not take up the majority of a talk, its influence is monumental. This is because it sets the tone of the entire message and affects the mood of the audience as well as of the speaker. I have listed seven tips to an effective introduction:

1. Look at your audience and pause. When used at the right time, silence can be a powerful tool for speakers. This is why it is a great idea to start off your talk by standing at the podium and looking out at your audience without saying anything. Make eye contact. Look over the whole congregation. This should only be done for about two or three seconds, but you will find that it is an excellent attention grabber.

2. Never start with negativity or an apology. I'm sure you have heard speakers begin talks with statements such as, "I have been so busy that I have not been able to prepare this talk as much as I would have liked." Or, "Well, the bishopric asked me to speak, and despite the fact that I don't like giving talks, I said I would speak today." Do you think such statements enhance the effectiveness of a talk? Of course they don't.

Nevertheless, many talks start off with some type of excuse or negative comment. Such statements have no place in any type of talk or lesson. They do nothing to enhance the speaker's goal or invite the Spirit. All that they do is discredit the speaker and lessen the effectiveness of the message being shared. If you're nervous, there's no need to mention it to everyone. This will only make the problem worse because it draws attention to any nervous behavior you may be exhibiting.

3. Be enthusiastic. Have you noticed that enthusiasm keeps coming up throughout this book? I cannot stress its importance enough. You don't have to start off your talks jumping up and down, yelling and screaming, but you do need to show that you are genuinely excited to have the opportunity to share your thoughts with a wonderful group of people.

Express your eagerness to share the message you have prepared. Tell the audience that you appreciate the opportunity to speak to them. Statements like these will establish an upbeat mood and initiate a sense of excitement among your listeners. These statements will also help to invite the influence of the Holy Ghost.

Notice this technique the next time you listen to a general conference address. Every speaker initiates his talk with some type of enthusiasm and appreciation.

4. Give your audience a preview of what they are going to hear. Just as previews of television programs or trailers for movies can excite an audience, you can excite your audience by giving a preview of what you are going to talk about. This can be done in just a few lines. Here's an example:

"I am excited to have this opportunity to speak to you on this wonderful day. I'm also thrilled to share with you a few experiences that I've had that have changed my life."

As you can see, this preview is basic and simple, but it gives the audience something to look forward to.

5. Share a little about yourself. This is especially a good idea when you're speaking to an audience that does not know a lot about you. By sharing with your listeners a few facts about yourself, you are able to build a relationship of trust with your audience and have the chance to affect them even more with the message you have prepared.

6. Bear your testimony. Sharing your testimony in the introduction of a talk can be an effective way to invite the Spirit. Saying a sentence as simple as "I testify in the name of Jesus Christ that the things I am going to speak about today are true" is powerful and will grab your audience's attention.

7. Sharing jokes at the beginning of a talk is not required. Although I do not oppose telling a joke at the beginning of a talk, there are other ways to break the ice with an audience. I usually prefer to share a funny or interesting story about myself. I have found this to be more effective than a joke because it is an icebreaker, attention-grabber, trust-builder, and tone-setter all in one.

THE BODY

In the previous chapter, we covered most aspects of what constitutes the body of an effective talk. As long as you use personal experiences or stories, show enthusiasm, and utilize scriptures and quotes, you should be effective. Remember to bear your testimony often, especially at the end of each story, and be sure to speak at the level of your listeners.

This also applies to the stories you share. Tell them in such a way that they can be beneficial to all listeners. Also, focus on members of the audience who seem most tuned in and interested in what you are saying. This will increase your confidence, concentration, and ability to speak effectively.

THE CONCLUSION

Your conclusion should be like your introduction—short but important. The conclusion is important because it is your last chance to make a great impact on your audience. I have listed four keys to an effective conclusion:

1. Always bear your testimony. Whether you have shared your testimony twenty times or not at all during the talk, always bear a strong testimony at the end. Say it with force and with power. Draw upon all of your faculties to express your testimony about your topic, the Savior, and his church.

2. Do not shuffle papers. I see this all the time, and I'm sure you do too. At the end of their talks, just when they are sharing their final testimonies, speakers begin to straighten up papers, close their scriptures, and stack everything in a pile. This not only distracts but also causes the speaker to look down at the podium instead of at the audience. The next time you give a talk, wait until you've said, "Amen." Then begin to put everything away.

3. Don't hesitate to share a final story, quote, or scripture. This is a good way to finish with a bang and leave your audience with something to remember. Accompany it with testimony, and you will have capped off an excellent talk with a powerful ending.

4. Leave your audience with a challenge. Throughout the talk, you have focused on having your audience understand a gospel principle more clearly. Now you want to leave your audience with some type of challenge that relates to the overall objective of your talk. As human beings, we love challenges. We thrive on them. Without them, we fall short of our potential. That is why every talk should consist of some type of challenge from the speaker.

You now have all of the information you need to produce a great talk. Apply what you have learned so far, and I promise that you will reap the benefits.

7

PRESIDENT MONSON'S SPEAKING METHODS

Now that we have covered the elements of a great talk, we're going to see these elements put to use by one of the most powerful and moving speakers in the Church today, President Thomas S. Monson. As I mentioned in chapter two, while preparing to write this book, I surveyed many members, asking them who their favorite speaker was. More than half named President Monson. After hearing so many positive comments about President Monson, I decided to take a closer look at his style and the characteristics of his talks. What I discovered supports everything we've talked about in this book.

To understand President Monson's style better, let's analyze a recent talk he gave during general conference titled "The Call to Serve" *(Ensign,* November 2000, 47–49). If you have access to this *Ensign,* I recommend that you read and study this talk.

Starting his address, President Monson states, "What a privilege is mine to stand before you tonight in this magnificent Conference Center and in assemblies throughout the world. What a mighty body of priesthood!"

You may have already noticed that a few attributes of this introduction coincide with the counsel given in this book. First, President Monson stresses that it is his "privilege" to speak to such an audience. Immediately, he puts himself on the same level as his listeners and expresses sincere gratitude for the opportunity to address them. President Monson also demonstrates his enthusiasm and passion in his introduction, saying, "What a mighty body of priesthood!"

After his initial statements, President Monson reads a scripture to give his talk direction and inform his listeners that he will be speaking on the priesthood. Following the scripture, he reads a quote by President Wilford Woodruff that discusses the power of the priesthood.

Before we continue analyzing this talk, let's review all that President Monson has done in just a few sentences. He has expressed appreciation to his audience and enthusiasm for his topic, he has read a scripture to give his talk direction, and he has shared a quote to add light to his topic.

Following the introduction, President Monson shares a personal experience about being ordained a deacon. He uses powerful details to generate interest. Immediately after sharing this experience, he bears his testimony to the young men and shares a quote from the Stanford University Memorial Church. (Notice how President Monson even gives the names of places, not just of people.) A few paragraphs later, he shares another story about a young man he knew as a bishop, whose name was Robert. The story involves Robert's triumph over his stuttering in order to perform the baptism of Nancy Ann McArthur.

Following this story about Robert, President Monson again bears his testimony as to the importance of providing youth with faith-promoting experiences. Throughout the remainder of the talk, President Monson shares two more personal experiences, one involving his first talk in church and another dealing with an experience he had while in the navy. He ends each story with his testimony.

What have we learned up to this point? First of all, we can see that President Monson has a great understanding of the power of personal experience. He knows that his audience will take interest in and relate to the stories he tells. He also understands that the best way to teach is by sharing what the world has taught him. He comprehends the importance of bearing his testimony at the right time.

To close his talk, President Monson shares a letter about President Hinckley that he received from a farmer. Before reading the letter, though, he gives his audience a preview of what they are about to hear: "I close by reading a simple yet profound letter that reflects our love for our prophet and his leadership." President Monson then shares the short, powerful letter, mentioning the name of the individual who wrote it. This leads him to his final statement, one of love and admiration, as he says, "President Hinckley, we the priesthood brethren of the Church do love and sustain you. I so testify, in the name of Jesus Christ, amen." What a beautiful conclusion to an incredible talk!

If someone wants to be a great speaker and teacher, all he needs to do is follow the example that President Monson has given in this talk. Throughout this book, I have reiterated that the characteristics of a great speaker are the ability to show enthusiasm, share personal experiences and stories, utilize scriptures and quotes, and form strong relationships with an audience. President Monson demonstrates all of these skills throughout his talk. He relates five personal experiences, reads three scriptures, and cites four quotes.

Chapter two contains a list of eleven keys to storytelling. In this talk, President Monson used ten of the keys. The only one he did not use was putting action into stories, which is pretty difficult when speaking at general conference. Chapter three contains five keys to sharing scriptures and quotes. President Monson used four of these keys.

Concerning the ten keys to a healthy audience-speaker relationship found in chapter four, President Monson used all ten! Now can you see what makes him such a great speaker? Most important, President Monson speaks with the Spirit.

The majority of President Monson's talks are just like the one we have analyzed in this chapter. He always demonstrates enthusiasm, tells powerful stories, utilizes scriptures and quotes, and forms a strong audience-speaker relationship. These qualities help make him one of the greatest speakers of this dispensation.

8
EFFECTIVE GOSPEL TEACHING

> *Now, at a time when our prophet is calling for more faith through hearing the word of God, we must revitalize and re-enthrone superior teaching in the Church.*
> —Jeffrey R. Holland

We have a challenge. Our challenge, at least from what Elder Jeffrey R. Holland has told us, is to become superior teachers of the gospel of Jesus Christ. How can we do this? And what exactly is effective gospel teaching? For starters, the Church tells us that the role of a gospel teacher is "to help individuals take responsibility for learning the gospel—to awaken in them the desire to study, understand, and live the gospel and to show them how to do so. . . . The learning has to be done by the pupil. Therefore it is the pupil who has to be put into action" (*Teaching: No Greater Call* [Salt Lake City: Deseret Book, 1999], 61).

Can we meet this challenge? Of course we can! And we will. This chapter is meant to help you to be the best teacher you can be. It consists of sixteen do's and five don'ts that are meant to guide you whenever you are blessed with the opportunity to teach a lesson in church or in life. Although we could probably write a whole book on the do's and don'ts of teaching, I want to stick with some of the basic keys that will lead to success.

It is also important to note that everything that we have talked about in this book can be applied to teaching lessons. The only major difference between a talk and a lesson is the fact that during a lesson, the audience participates more and the teacher speaks less. Also, remember that the key to any great lesson is the influence of the Holy Spirit on the teacher and the class members.

THE SIXTEEN DO'S OF TEACHING AN EFFECTIVE GOSPEL LESSON

1. Show enthusiasm. Here we go again with the E-word. We can never talk enough about the importance of enthusiasm. Teachers must be enthusiastic and passionate about their topics. That is what keeps students awake, on the edge of their seats, and excited to come to class.

2. Talk less. I have seen many great speakers give ineffective lessons. Why? Because teachers often forget that class members are there to participate, not just to listen. In order for everyone in a class to be edified, all must participate in some way. This cannot occur if the teacher is speaking the whole time. In fact, a teacher should talk less than 50 percent of the time to ensure maximum classroom participation.

3. Always have a clear idea of the lesson's objective, and stick to it (unless the Spirit indicates otherwise). Everything that is done or said in your lesson should in some way deal with your lesson objective. If someone, including the teacher, gets off track, the lesson will lose focus and become less effective. This often happens when a class member digresses. Although this cannot always be prevented, it is your duty as the teacher to get everyone back on track.

4. Prepare diligently and prayerfully. If you are not prepared, your class members will recognize this immediately and may lose interest in the lesson. You want to give them the impression that you have worked hard to prepare for the message you are about to share. This impression leads to respect and more effort from the class.

Also, take advantage of the power of prayer. By doing this, the Lord will enlighten you as to what you need to do and say to help the members of your class.

5. Ask thought-provoking questions that invite discussion. The greatest teachers are the ones that let class members teach themselves. You accomplish this when you ask thought-provoking questions. (Stay away from "yes" and "no" questions). When you ask questions, sometimes it's a good idea to ask a specific class member to respond. Although you don't want to embarrass anyone, some students need a little motivation to participate.

6. Show love and appreciation. Love will always be a great motivator and teacher.

7. Use stories and examples. As previously mentioned, if you have learned something from an experience, your class members will likely learn from your experience as well.

8. Use pictures and objects. It's a fact that the human mind remembers pictures and objects much better than it does words.

9. Use activities. Activities are great because they stimulate learning by providing a change of pace for class members.

10. Bear your testimony often. It's important to bear your testimony throughout the lesson, not just at the end. A teacher can also ask class members to bear their testimonies on a certain topic. This is a great way of inviting the influence of the Holy Ghost.

11. Always provide students with positive feedback. No matter what point a student raises, it's your job to respond in some type of positive manner. This will increase class participation. Some examples of possible responses to a class member's comments are:

- Thanks for the comment.
- I like how you put that.
- That sounds interesting.
- You bring up an important point.
- Let's see what the scriptures tell us about this matter.

- Could you explain further?
- I think I'll write that one down!
- What a great idea!
- Now we're thinking!

12. Know your class members. As a teacher, you should do your best to know the names of your class members and other pertinent information about them that will help you to motivate them to learn and apply what they learn. Also, the more interest you show in your class members, the more interest they will have in the things you teach.

13. Teach at the level of your audience. We talked about this in chapter four. Great teachers know how to adjust their lessons according to the levels of their class members.

14. Always review with class members what they have learned. It is a great idea to do this at the beginning and end of each lesson. At the beginning of your lessons, ask class members what they learned during the previous lesson. Also, ask if they have applied anything they learned from that lesson. At the end of each lesson, ask class members what they have learned and what they will be taking with them once class ends.

15. Ask for feedback from class members. One must have thick skin in order to do this, but with thick skin comes self-improvement. Your class members, especially if they are youth, are usually willing to give you feedback on your teaching skills. Ask them what you do well. Find out what you could do better.

16. Follow the Church lesson manual. The Church

has produced many wonderful lesson manuals so that we, as members, can have more productive classes. There is no reason to "wing it" with our own information.

THE FIVE DON'TS OF EFFECTIVE LESSON TEACHING

1. Don't make excuses or apologize. No one has ever been uplifted by hearing a teacher say he didn't have enough time during the week to prepare a lesson. Making such a statement is like saying, "I have many priorities and this class is just not one of them." If you have made the mistake of poor preparation, keep it to yourself.

2. Don't bury your face in a lesson manual. If you are looking for a surefire way to bore your class members to death, just look down at your teaching manual and read from it the whole lesson. This provides little opportunity for creativity, enthusiasm, and class participation.

3. Don't demean or embarrass class members. No one wants to be embarrassed. Embarrassment and hurt feelings are what cause members to go inactive. Embarrassment causes hard feelings, and when hard feelings are present, the Spirit is absent.

4. Don't preach your own doctrine. Being a teacher in the Church does not authorize you to share your opinions on doctrines for which the Church has not offered elaboration. Stick with the basic facts of the gospel. For example, if you're giving a lesson on the Second Coming, don't tell your class when you think the Second Coming is going to happen. To say that the time is near is fine, but to say that it will happen in 2020 will

PARADISE
TO THE RESCUE

A series of real-life stories illustrating the good, the bad
and sometimes ugly reality of dog rescue in a small
town in rural Spain.

This book is dedicated to everyone involved
in animal rescue

Front Cover Image

TONY

A long-term resident of PARADISE still waiting
for his forever home

This is a remarkable book and shows the compassion, love and kindness that goes into rescuing these wonderful animals.

Such good work is being done.

These stories should be read by all of us dog lovers and everyone who cares about our beloved pets. Also, it should be required reading for those who treat them badly and need to be educated and enlightened.

Lorraine Kelly, OBE

Contents

The harsh reality of rescue

Introduction by Dr LESLEY HUNTER

I have been a dog owner for most of my life and have had the privilege of working with many wonderful professionals ranging from veterinary specialists to animal behaviourists and Police dog trainers. However, when I was asked to support Paradise Rescue Kennels, by editing and publishing this book, my first thought was … but I haven't rescued a dog. In fact, all my animals have been bought specifically to be family pets, so what did I really know about rescue and adoption, let alone doing this in Spain?

Since 2016, I have had the privilege of being able to spend some time in our holiday home in the Costa Blanca. On these occasions, I have either been accompanied by our elderly German Shepherd (who sadly passed away while in Spain) or, more recently, by our current German Shepherd puppy who loves having his own swimming pool. We have met so many people who have adopted dogs from local animal shelters that I decided to investigate why there were so many animals in such need … the findings are not comfortable but I have reached one definite conclusion – my next dog will be a rescue!

There are many reasons why dogs can find themselves in a rescue situation, but typically they are either abandoned deliberately or are lost. Abandonment is a major animal welfare problem in Spain. It is virtually impossible to locate accurate and reliable national figures but the trend that is consistently reported across the media is that the number of

1

dogs taken into shelters has remained relatively constant for the past four years[1,2]. A recent whitepaper, produced by the research organisation Fundación Affinity[3], estimates that **104,688** dogs were taken in by animal shelters in Spain in 2018 alone. This is considered to be a conservative estimate and the actual number could be significantly higher. The research also suggests that medium and large sized dogs are more likely to be abandoned, while nearly a quarter of all dogs are abandoned as very young puppies. This is particularly worrying and has a number of implications for rescue shelters, including:

- The cost of having to fund the rearing of puppies, including medical checks, vaccinations and microchipping.
- The need to isolate young puppies from other established dogs in shelters.
- The 24/7 demands of young puppies.
- The fact that older dogs are often overlooked for adoption in preference for the cuter puppies.

Owning a dog is a commitment that should never be taken lightly and every dog owner should clearly understand their role and duty to demonstrate responsible ownership. Failure to do this typically leads to one of the five main reasons why dogs are abandoned in Spain.

1. Pregnancy and unwanted litters of puppies.
2. Behavioural issues (particularly in large breeds).
3. Financial factors – veterinary care and feeding costs.
4. Loss of interest, for instance in exercising and caring for the dog.
5. Seasonal factors, such as the end of the hunting season in Spain.

Despite many Spaniards being dog lovers and responsible owners, the scale of the animal welfare problem in Spain remains a particular cause for concern, especially since the available figures suggest that the number of adoptions has remained similar for the past five years. As puppies continue to dominate the adoption choice, more older dogs are destined to spend the remainder of their lives in rescue centres. Many shelters struggle with overcrowding and this situation can only get worse as more older, larger dogs continue to become long term residents.

Paradise Rescue Kennels

Paradise Rescue Kennels is an established dog rescue centre in Benferri in the Costa Blanca region of Spain. It is privately owned and run by Colleen Jay and her husband, Peter, and relies entirely on donations and fund-raising to operate.

Twenty years ago, after rescuing donkeys for many years in Ireland, Colleen and Peter moved to Spain, with the intention of retiring. Peter initially built Paradise Rescue Kennels as a hobby for Colleen. It was meant to be half for boarding and half for rescue. The boarding dogs were intended to fund the rescues but it rapidly became all rescue and started to rely on donations to keep it going. It soon became clear that Peter would need to build more kennel runs and the number expanded until it reached the 28 runs that are currently at Paradise today. Alongside these, 10 Isolation Kennels and a Puppy House have been established to give the capacity to house 80 to 100 dogs and puppies at any given time.

Paradise mainly rescues dogs throughout the Alicante and Murcia regions of Spain, although recent years has seen an increase in rescuing dogs 'at the last minute' from animal kill stations in other parts of the country.

Paradise has built an enviable reputation in the local area and benefits from the loyalty of a dedicated group of supporters committed to ensuring that all the dogs receive the best experiences and opportunities, regardless of their age, background or reason for residing at Paradise. One of the most notable features is that the people who get involved with Paradise feel they become part of the *Paradise Family*. This often leads to foster placements becoming adoptions, and initial single adoptions leading to subsequent serial adoptions of multiple dogs. Although many of these adoptions happen locally in Spain, a significant number of previous Paradise residents are now living in their forever homes in countries as far afield as UK, Belgium, Norway, Sweden, Luxembourg, Finland and The Netherlands.

The successful adoption rate at Paradise is a testament to the hard work and tireless efforts of Colleen's core volunteer, Mary-Ann Dunning, who is often posting appeals on Facebook at the early hours of the morning after a day spent collecting dogs from horrendous conditions or sitting anxiously in the waiting rooms of the local vets.

This book is a collection of stories and case studies that highlight the appalling conditions in which many such dogs have been found but also illustrates the transformation that can happen when Paradise supporters have adopted them into their hearts and homes. It is an attempt to raise awareness, and I am particularly grateful to Mary-Ann for her insights and stories, and to all contributors for sharing their experiences and photographs of their dogs.

In recent weeks, just prior to the publication of this book, our area of Spain suffered a tragedy caused by torrential storms and flooding attributed to The Gota Fria 2019. Sadly, the devastating effects of heavy rain caused severe flooding as local rivers burst their banks. Roads became impassable, thousands of people were evacuated, homes were destroyed and, tragically, several people lost their lives in catastrophic circumstances. Paradise, like many other animal shelters, suffered tremendous damage that will take time to repair … but the dogs are all safe and new residents continue to arrive with alarming frequency.

It is wonderful to read about dogs that have had their lives turned around by a little love and some tender care, but please do not get carried away with the feel good factor. The problem of dog abandonment in Spain is not going away any time soon. We can only do our own little bit in whatever way is right for each of us individually – but every little helps – so thank you for reading and for caring.

Spanish Breeds

There are many different dog breeds in Spain but the three main ones that are most commonly represented in animal shelters are Galgos, Podencos and Mastins (or different variations on a Mastin cross). In Paradise, the typical profile of the longer term residents is 25% Galgo, 15% Podenco, another 15% Mastin and the remaining 45% a variety of different breeds and crossbreeds.

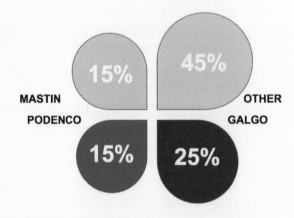

Each of these breeds has its own unique characteristics and it is therefore important for any potential adopter to understand their specific needs.

Galgo

Galgos are often referred to as 'Spanish Greyhounds' and are a member of the sighthound family. Despite their name, and similarity in appearance, they are not closely related to the English Greyhound. Galgos are typically slightly higher in the rear than the front and also tend to be smaller and lighter in build. They have a long tail, a long streamlined head and large ears.

Galgos can be smooth or rough coated and come in various colours:
- Barcino or atigrado – Brindle
- Negro – Black
- Barquillo – Golden
- Tostado – Toasted
- Canela – Cinnamon
- Amarillo – Yellow
- Rojo – Red
- Blanco – White
- Berrendo – White with patches
- Pio – Any colour with white muzzle and forehead

Galgos are built for speed and endurance and are therefore often bred specifically to be used in hunting, hare coursing and racing. Despite this, they have a calm temperament and are usually friendly to other dogs and cats and are often gentle with children. They can be shy and reserved of new things, people and places so need to have carefully planned socialisation from an early age.

Galgos are medium to big dogs with a typical lifespan of 12 to 15 years. A male dog will usually weigh between 25kg to 30kg and a female can weigh 20kg to 25kg. They need exercise to run regularly but, between these bursts of high intensity activity, a Galgo's favourite place is a comfy sofa and you are likely to find them fast asleep with their legs in the air doing a strange Yoga position.

Podenco

The origins of this breed can be traced back to Ancient Egypt but today, the Spanish Podenco is typically bred and used for hunting rabbits. They are multi-sensory hunting dogs and are characterised by their highly mobile ears, which are usually held erect.

Podencos come in various sizes, colours and coats that are often defined by region. Male rabbit hunting Podencos (Podenco Andaluz, Canario, Ibizenco, Mallorquin and Menorquin) typically weight up to 23kg with females slightly lighter around 19kg. The much larger Podenco Campanero can reach weights in excess of 60kg and is used for hunting deer and wild boar.

Podencos are loyal and make a loving family dog. They are extremely friendly and sociable with other dogs. Podencos have lots of energy and need plenty of exercise and long walks. They are very agile and can jump from standing; when in pursuit of prey, they have even been known to climb trees! As an owner of a Podenco you need at least a six-foot fence and secure outdoor area.

Mastin

The Mastin Español is a breed of giant purebred dogs in Spain but these are relatively rare. Most Mastins found in rescue centres are crossbreeds and are typically any large dog that has a significant Mastin component. Mastins usually weigh at least 35kg – 40kg but can reach as much as 100kg when fully grown.

Mastins are instantly recognisable from their unique physical appearance. They are big heavily built dogs with a broad chest, a fatty pouch (dewlap) on their neck and drooping (lop) ears. They can be any colour, or range of colours, but are usually a mix of reds, browns and white.

Mastíns were originally bred in Spain to guard livestock making them independent and vigilant. They interact well with other dogs and love to play, although they can be clumsy and intimidating due to their size.

Mastins are affectionate and very loyal to people they know but can be a little aloof and stand-offish with strangers until they learn to trust them.

Message from Mary-Ann

My Paradise story by MARY-ANN DUNNING

There's a mixture of satisfaction, elation, worry and a huge sense of relief when a process comes together. It's hard to describe the feeling when the kennel has taken in a dog, rehabilitated it and then found a home where the dog adopters will love the dog as much as we have. Colleen has seen hundreds of dogs leave Paradise and still feels that excitement – maybe if we give you an insight into kennel life, you'll understand why.

There is a cage outside our gate. We know that dogs will be left, so it is there in the hope that they will be left inside it. The kennels seem miles from anywhere but the nearby road can be busy and is a risk to any stray. Colleen has actually witnessed cars screech to a halt and a dog being thrown out of an open door. After 20 years, the '*dog lady*' and her kennels have become well known. We've been asked why we don't have cameras at the gate but why would we? Sadly, we know that this deterrent would ensure that the dogs would simply be abandoned to an uncertain future elsewhere.

Paradise runs a Charity Shop in La Murada and locally this has become known as the '*shop for dogs*'. Frequently this is too literal and dogs are brought in and simply left as if they were a bag of old clothes. Colleen can regularly be seen hand feeding puppies while trying to attend to customers.

We are used to the excuses given for handing in dogs but the most surprising yet is the little dog who was brought in to be put to sleep, because the family were allergic to her, yet within hours she had given birth! Nothing surprises us.

We have received dogs so traumatised by past experiences that we fear there will never be a happy future for them. We have had dogs with scars, sometimes still weeping from the wire around their neck or the burns to their skin. We have taken dogs that have been dragged behind cars in an attempt to increase their speed, their pads ripped to shreds. But every time a dog arrives at Paradise … they are safe, secure and stand a fighting chance.

Colleen has spent a lifetime of going without to ensure that the animals in her care have the best possible chance in life, she keeps going for the love of dogs. At 69 years of age, she is up every day at the crack of dawn and works till dusk in both the kennels and our Charity Shop. She simply won't say no to any dog in distress. She rescues throughout Alicante and Murcia and has also taken dogs out of kill stations in other parts of the country. She's been knee deep in mud, rescued dogs trapped in drains, in bins and it is a regular occurrence to open the gate in the morning to be greeted by a box of puppies or dogs tied to the fence.

It is often a juggling act because we are always at capacity but somehow we always find room. When the pens are all full, the Isolation Kennels are full and Colleen's bedrooms are full, there's still a little space somewhere for a dog in need. We have a lot of sleepless nights worrying about our puppies and adult dogs. We have so many long term residents at Paradise and our fear is always that if a puppy fails to attract an adopter at it's cute and cuddly stage, as it grows and becomes too big for the Puppy House, then it will become invisible among so many other adult dogs.

Countering this is that feeling I've already mentioned, when a plan comes together and the right home is found – a sense of satisfaction, elation and relief. The worry drops away and a buzz drives you on through the ups and downs of the rescues that follow and what they entail.

Many rescue kennels get funding but Paradise is entirely run on donations, fundraising activities and the takings from our Charity Shop. Times have been incredibly hard for Colleen and on occasions, when the kennels are overflowing, the vet bills are piling up, a lesser person would have thrown in the towel … but not Colleen. The amazing supporters that Paradise has always dig deep. The funds raised to purchase the kennel van and to complete the upgrade and recent refurbishment of the dog pens are testament to their generosity and loyalty to Paradise.

The main tool for finding homes for our dogs is the use of social media. We have followers in many countries and our main Facebook account is like a big family chat page. We have wonderful supporters who love to share the antics of their Paradise dogs and, while we promote our dogs for adoption here, we also have a Facebook group that is solely to find homes for our current kennel dogs.

Thank you for all your loyalty and support – you are always there when we need you.

BAZA BABES

How my day in Paradise lasted for 72 hours! It just started with a message, nothing much out of the ordinary, but the chain of events that followed was pretty life changing.

Baza Babes

Story by MARY-ANN DUNNING

I had been a volunteer dog walker at Paradise for a couple of years and, on the odd occasion, had transported dogs just to help out. When the message arrived, I was preparing the car ready to take two Galgos to their new home in San Javier. It was from a Scandinavian lady who had rescued four mistreated German Shepherd puppies and wanted to know if we could take them. They had been with their parents, one of whom was being beaten. They were all living in a yard behind a restaurant. The owner had allowed her to take the puppies and she said she was going back for the adults.

As things turned out, the stars were aligned for these little puppies. They too were in San Javier and the lady had very kindly said that if we took them, she would pay for all their injections, passports and ultimate rehoming in her own country. This was all too good to be true … so arrangements were quickly made to include the puppies in my trip.

The drop off and the pick-up went very smoothly and with the puppies installed in the flat below our house, I set to on the Paradise Facebook page to see if anyone could foster these little sweethearts. As if by magic, up popped great friend of Paradise and dog behaviourist, Nicki, happy to foster for three months.

15

My first encounter with Nicki was when I had met her near her home in Almeria. I had taken one of our mentally tortured Shepherds (Tara) in the hope that she could rehabilitate her. Nicki was marvellous with her and we were delighted that it became a failed foster and, to this day, Tara is never far from her side. This little meet-up was going to be different, however. Nicki was now living on top of a mountain on the far side of Granada. A mere 800 km round trip! Distance has never been an object, so off I set with a cage full of travel sick puppies on our long journey. It was a labour of love and so nice to spend the night at Nicki and her husband's wonderful home.

The next morning, I was up with the larks and, after breakfast and a quick goodbye to the puppies, I prepared myself for the drive back down the mountain track.

The leisurely journey home should run smoothly. Beautiful scenery to look at, no pressure to meet any deadlines, just a nice little saunter through beautiful Andalusia … but then the first message arrived, and the second, then many more followed by a call from Colleen.

"Will you be driving near Baza?"

Just the mention of that name sends shivers through even the toughest dog rescuer. Baza – a killing station – stark and open to the elements with no security. A horrible place where killing day is a Friday … and this was a Friday!

As the story unfolded, WhatsApp messages began flying round. Five Galgo puppies were about to be killed but now there was hope if someone from Paradise could be there by closure at 1pm. Oh my goodness, that would be me … the pressure was on!

It is well documented that I have received more than one traffic violation whilst on Paradise business, but with my foot to the floor all I could think of was these little Galgo puppies against whom the clock was ticking.

It was a panic once I reached Baza with a satnav that had no idea where I was going and my poor Spanish stretched to the limit. I finally found the white concrete walls … drove past it … drove round it … drove through it … but could see no sign of life. A horrible sick feeling came over me as I spotted the dying embers of what had clearly been a large bonfire … was I too late? As I left my car and walked past all the empty pens my stomach was churning – were the puppies still alive?

At last I heard the sound of an engine and along came my contact but there was no welcome here. The man took me past many pens which looked recently used and then I saw them! I felt such relief. These puppies would now stand a chance.

Between us, the man and I took them back to my car and once they were safely installed in the cage, I asked for the mandatory form to be signed. When he simply said "No" and disappeared, I was totally confused. I couldn't fathom out what was happening - where had he gone?

The answer soon became clear as he, accompanied by a surly sidekick, returned carrying more puppies! In broken English, he explained that no form would be signed unless I also took these little ones!

I had no choice … without us both signing the form, I couldn't rescue the Galgos and, unless I added these fluffy little things to the cage, there would be no form and no release of any of the puppies.

Put them in the cage …
Just put them in the cage …
I had to get away from this place …
Put them in the cage!

Driving away from Baza I had to break the news to Colleen. I had no idea how many little bodies were scuffling round in the back of my car, but at least they were now safe and on their way to Paradise.

It was dark and late by the time I arrived back at the kennels. Colleen had prepared a large pen in the isolation part of the Puppy House and one by one we popped them in and settled them for the night.

Twelve puppies.
I'd brought back twelve puppies!

In the cold light of the following day, we looked in the Puppy House to see what we actually had. No worse for their journey, there was a frenzy of activity to greet us. We had a mix of classic Galgos and some quite furry Lurcher cross Galgos – six, not five – and then the extra little batch of non-specific fluffy bundles.

Ellie, my predecessor at Paradise, had so many other puppies and adult dogs to rehome, that I decided I would take responsibility for these little souls. I'll put them on the Facebook page and find homes – simple. However, my inexperience became quickly obvious. The non-Galgo puppies were very tiny so I pitched them as likely to be the size of a Jack Russell but then they grew and they grew and they grew! Subsequently the adopters of two of the litter had DNA tests done which indicated a cocktail of Pyrenean, German Shepherd and Spanish Greyhound (Galgo). They were a stunning litter that very quickly attracted attention but they were very big!

The wonderful thing about our Paradise supporters is that they are always there when we need them and suddenly this was such a time. We now had 12 extra puppies to add to those already in the Puppy House and there was a big 'let down' on its way. On my journey to and from Granada, I had been trying to contact the little German Shepherd's benefactor but her lack of response was causing me concern and that's when the message arrived. She was apparently very sorry but not only would she not be funding the vaccinations and passports for the puppies, but there would be no transport to their new, evidently non-existent homes.

Sadly I had been scammed but at least the puppies were safe.

Now I needed a plan! I decided to apply the 12-month rule. If it is still in the box unused after 12 months … then you don't need it. I had bought my husband a Kindle for his birthday and it was still in the box. I would raffle it online to help pay for the puppies' injections – I had my plan. The wonderful friends of Paradise rallied to the call and the vet bills that

Nicki had accrued would now be covered. It was my first attempt at fundraising and it was a success.

Now for the next challenge.
What do I call sixteen puppies?

Four female German Shepherds … The Spice Girls of course! Saffron, Mace, Cinnamon and Nutmeg who very quickly attracted attention and adopters were soon found. Mace (Macey) was the first to go and off she went on the transport to Huddersfield in the UK. Saffron (Saffey) was next and joined her new family at a nearby Camp Site in Spain. They had driven down from the Costa Brava and would be taking her back to their lovely rural home.

Cinnamon was renamed Ava and Nutmeg (now Eller) both went to homes quite near to Paradise and have continued to meet up for walks together. All four, happily settled in loving homes. Four down, 12 to go …

The 12 puppies from Baza Killing Station now needed some names. A couple were earmarked and named before I'd put my thinking cap on but, unfortunately through the harsh reality of rescue, one of the little babies didn't make it. The remain nine were all stars so I christened them with the glamorous names they deserved although most people change the name of their pet once it has been adopted, which can be very confusing at times!

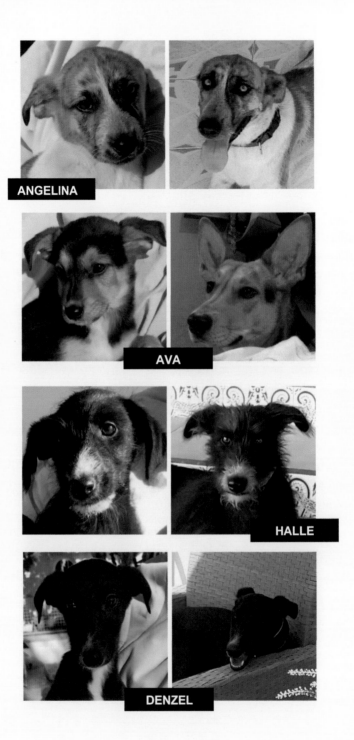

ANGELINA

AVA

HALLE

DENZEL

21

SYLVESTER

SOPHIA

CEDRIC

CLINT & SCARLETT

22

It might not be easy, but very little is in animal rescue, so once again, with the power of social media, a few sleepless nights and a lot of organisation, my new "career" had begun. It started as a quick drive to the coast, up a mountain and then 72 hours later, back to my home.

Eventually, with adopters for every one of the puppies, I could now get a sense of what drives Colleen on and, in a small way, I felt I could now say that I was part of the ups and downs of dog rescue.

Abandoned in the gutter

Lana

Adopted by
CAROL HANBY

Lana

Introduction by MARY-ANN DUNNING

In December 2017, Coleen was driving through La Murada when she caught a glimpse of movement in a gutter. It was little old Elena, curled up, trying to keep warm. People were passing by her without a second glance but she was quickly scooped up and secured safely in Colleen's van.

Once back at the kennels she checked for a microchip. The good news … she had one. The bad news … when Colleen rang the number, the man who answered denied ownership and wanted nothing to do with her. Little Elena had been abandoned and left all alone in the gutter!

The vet estimated that Elena was about 11 years old. She was a lovely friendly dog but no one in Spain wanted to foster or adopt a little oldie …

Lana's story by CAROL HANBY

Paradise kept promoting her on Facebook and, in the following June, I spotted her! By the summer, Elena (renamed Lana) was heading for her new life and forever home in the UK.

Lana now lives happily in Saddleworth, a beautiful moorland region in the North west of England, with a parrot, a budgie and her best friend 'Taz' the Pug who visits regularly.

Lana has taught me how rewarding rescuing a dog can be. She loves being part of a family and responds to lots of love. Lana has changed my life for the better, I am healthier from all the exercise, I have an animal best friend and I get lots of love mirrored back to me, it's great.

My advice to anyone thinking of adoption is simple. If you are sure you have time to spend with a pet, don't hesitate, just do it!

"

Dogs are not our
whole life, but they
make our lives
whole.

- ROGER CARAS

Thrown down a well

Marley

Adopted by
ELLIE SUSSEX

Marley

Introduction by MARY-ANN DUNNING

The Spanish owner of a house close to Paradise sadly died, but when the family cleared it in preparation for the new occupants, they didn't know what to do with the two little dogs that had been left … so they threw them down the well on the property!

Days later the new occupants heard whimpering and discovered Marley lying at the bottom with his little friend, who by that time had sadly died.

Marley's story by ELLIE SUSSEX

It was early 2014 and I had only popped over to Paradise Kennels to help with the weekly dog walking. As soon as I saw his big brown eyes something sparked in me. It was like love at first woof. I just felt this instant connection and was immediately head over heels in love with him.

As soon as he arrived at the house, he made himself at home. After some rather wacky name suggestions from the kids like "*Jesus*" and "*Dr Who*" we finally all settled on *Marley.*

Marley had been with Colleen at Paradise Kennels for four years after being found. To this day, Marley is scared of the dark. He is shy around men but has the most amazing relationship with the kids – he loves to sit with them while they are reading and will always be an ear to listen when they want to talk.

We lived in Spain with Marley for nearly four years and have recently moved to Epsom Downs in Surrey. Marley travelled well to the UK and he will now see out his sunset years in lush green fields watching the kids grow up.

Every rescue dog has a story and they will try and tell you in their own way. Marley's issues were the dark and shyness of men. But we are working hard to overcome this with a simple table lamp at night and my husband slowly, but surely, winning his trust with lots of treats and walks to the pub!

It has been an absolute pleasure to adopt Marley. A rescue dog has so much love to give and our family is proud for him to be one of us. Everyone thinks their dog is the best … and they are right … every dog is the best … but to our family, Marley is our one in a million dog.

For anyone thinking of adoption, my advice would be to trust your gut. If you see that special dog (in person or a photo on a rehoming site) and you feel a connection to them, then trust it.

TWINKLE

This little dog had touched all of our hearts and the whole family was in total agreement that we wanted Twinkle to stay with us as her forever home.

ADOPTED BY LESLEY SALMON

Twinkle

Introduction by MARY-ANN DUNNING

Twinkle is a pure bred English Setter and was originally owned by a hunter in Spain. At the age of about eight weeks, she was taken to a local vet in La Murada to be put to sleep as she had been attacked by another dog and suffered serious injuries – her right eye was literally hanging out onto her chest and her lip had also been torn.

They say things happen for a reason and at that precise moment who should walk into the veterinary clinic but the totally amazing Colleen! Raffa the vet immediately took Colleen to see Twinkle who, without hesitation, told Raffa to do whatever needed to be done agreeing that she would pay and then look after Twinkle.

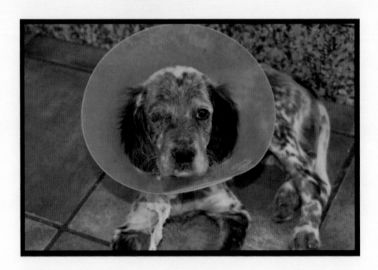

Twinkle arrived at the kennels with her eye and lip stitched and wearing a cone to protect her face – she needed special looking after and a foster home.

Twinkle's story by LESLEY SALMON

I support Paradise and try to help Colleen by walking some of the dogs. One day Twinkle appeared from the house and Colleen aimed a big smile directly at me saying that she needed a foster home – how could I say no? Twinkle was soon in the car to meet my three other dogs. They were not sure what to make of her – Twinkle likes to get in your face for a lick and a cuddle – and they were faced with this wriggly, waggy tailed puppy with a cone on her head who kept bashing them with it!

I needed to keep an eye on her, so Twinkle was made a bed beside mine and from that day to this she has never had an accident in the house. In fact, if she does need to go out in the night she goes around the other side and jumps up on the bed to wake my husband up!

Although she settled quickly, after a few days Twinkle clearly wasn't herself. She started to be sick and was drinking but not eating. I wasn't sure what to do so rang Colleen at Paradise who advised I take her straight to the local animal hospital at Guadamar. When we got there they did a test and immediately told us that Twinkle had 'parvo' and that it would be touch and go whether she would make it. I had only had this little girl a week at the most but I was already hopelessly in love and to say I was devasted was such an under exaggeration. I left her in the capable hands of the vet but had the worst night of my life worrying about her.

The following morning there was no change and that afternoon I went to visit fully expecting that it might be to say goodbye. When I saw her, she was obviously so poorly but when she heard my voice her tail managed just the slightest of wags. Another day passed and then I had a phone call from the vet. Fearing the worst, I was totally over the moon when the nurse said …

Can you please come and get your dog as she is barking and making too much noise!

Twinkle was so much better that it was time to start thinking about putting her up for adoption. I tried to be strong about it but the thought of her going to live somewhere else was not good at all. She had offers of a home from all over Europe and even an enquiry from America.

This little dog had touched all of our hearts and the whole family was in total agreement that we wanted Twinkle to stay with us as her forever home.

At first, things were perfect with Twinkle but after a few weeks we noticed she wasn't herself again and some lesions has started to appear on her face. So off we went on another trip to the vet …

This dog is so gentle and mild mannered – she loves everyone – unless you are a vet and then she changes into a barking demon dog! I am not sure if she remembers from when she had parvo or recalls when she had eye surgery. I don't know but her reaction makes it very difficult for her to be treated and she does have a really deep very loud bark!

Initially, the vet thought Twinkle was having an allergic reaction and gave us some cream and tablets. However, over the next few weeks, she continued to get worse until it was suggested that she be tested for Leishmaniasis; a parasitic disease transmitted to dogs by infected Sand-flies.

The test for Leishmaniasis came back positive!

We were all devastated but, in a way also relieved, because we now had a label and a cause of Twinkle's decline. The treatment is best described as like having chemotherapy. It is very strong and is administered wearing gloves. Fortunately my angel doesn't mind in the slightest and happily takes her medicine. Gradually over the course of a month things started to improve – her hair stopped falling out, the lesions started to heal and our Twinkle was literally coming back to life in front of our eyes.

Twinkle is now two years old and is the most special dog with a huge personality and a love of life. She needs to take medicine every day to keep the disease under control and, at the moment, it is working really well. She is healthy, happy and a joy to be around. She will have another blood test at the end of the year to check her progress …

Abandoned in the mountains

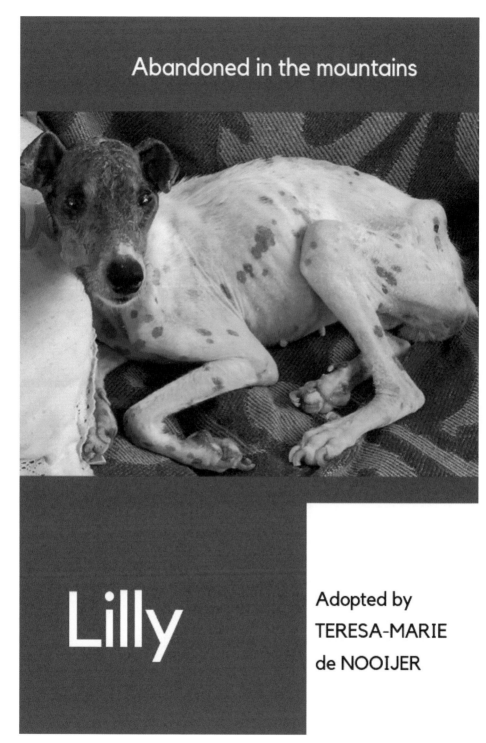

Lilly

Adopted by
TERESA-MARIE
de NOOIJER

Lilly

Introduction by MARY-ANN DUNNING

There are many days when we have tears on the terrace
and the day that little Lilly arrived was one of those days.
Abandoned up in the mountains this little Bodagero had both
Leishmaniasis and Lyme Disease and was seriously
emaciated and very ill. I was called up to the terrace to see if
I could take a video of her because the others hadn't
managed. Ellie and Colleen had both tried but failed. It was
only when I saw her alongside Colleen and Ellie, both in
floods of tears, that I realised why they couldn't.

"I can do this", I thought, but as I bobbed down and focused
my phone on her little face, I felt I could see into her soul.
Her eyes in that instant were pleading for me to tell her that
everything would be all right and that she was safe now and

the pain would go away. But I couldn't do that because there were now three of us on the terrace sobbing our eyes out. Eventually on the fifth attempt, I managed to stop my voice from wobbling and the video was filmed. We needed to advertise the fact that we had this precious soul and that special care was needed for her. Her body and face were covered in sores. She needed medication but, above all, she needed tender, loving care.

I quickly put a post on our Facebook page asking if there was a foster home out there and within the day little Lilly was safe in the arms of Teresa-Marie de Nooijer, one of our loyal supporters. She and Mick Blackwell would foster Ellie and try to build her up and hopefully give her a chance at a future.

It is a well-known fact that we at Paradise love to see a failed foster and, to our delight, this was one of them. Within a couple of days, there was no way that Teresa and Mick would give little Lilly to anyone. She was now part of the family and was there to stay.

Lilly now lives the dream with Poodle (Maya), Rhodesian Ridgeback (Nala) and Paradise Rescue (Jet). Such a far cry from near death in the mountains.

We only cry happy tears for Lilly now.

Lilly's story by Teresa- Marie de Nooijer

Lilly was such a fragile little dog when I first met her but, to have survived this far, she had to be a determined, wonderful little battler. All she needed was some love and tender care to overcome the pain and discomfort of her horrible diseases. It took time but she has thrived. The diseases are thankfully in remission, her weight and strength have built up and she now enjoys running and playing with her extended canine family.

Lilly loves the beach but her real passion is Agility – she is so eager to please and has an amazing strength of spirit that shines through – I am so proud of her!

Dumped in a cardboard box

Sophie

Adopted by
SHEILA & PETER
STANDLEY

Sophie

Introduction by MARY-ANN DUNNING

The gate bell rang one evening while Colleen was cleaning the Puppy House. By the time she got there and opened the gate, all she saw were tail lights disappearing down the track. Strange … until she looked down and there, in front of her, was a box of puppies!

Sophie was one of these puppies, dumped like unwanted litter in a cardboard box.

Sophie's story by Sheila & Peter Standley

When we first brought Sophie home, she was so tiny! She could run underneath our other dog (Patch) but she had the most amazing huge ears. She bonded with Patch very quickly, in fact she has brought out the puppy in him. She grew very quickly, her legs just got longer and longer and now Patch can run under her.

She loves going for family walks and usually manages to cover many more miles than the rest of us. She is like a gazelle when she runs and covers the ground very quickly.

Sophie is mischievous but her guilty look often gives her away. She has chewed her way through several flip-flops and she flattens her ears and slinks off to her bed when she knows she is in trouble. She is the first to greet you when you have been out and is always so pleased to see you, leaping up and down and wagging her stumpy tail.

Sophie has travelled hundreds of miles by car and ship to the UK and back and slept in various hotels on the way. She loves to be with people and is happiest curled up on the sofa with her forever family.

My advice is that when you take on a rescue dog, have patience, they will reward you with so much more. Sophie and Patch are the best of friends now – they are both so comical and many of their antics have had us in stitches laughing.

66

Dogs do speak, but only to those who know how to listen.

- ORHAN PAMUK

BLOSSOM

It had been a long time coming and it was a day that we in dog rescue had looked forward to with optimism.

ADOPTED BY MARY-ANN DUNNING

Blossom

Blossom's story by MARY-ANN DUNNING

February 1st 2018. It had been a long time coming and it was a day that we in dog rescue had looked forward to with optimism. It was the day that the new Animal Protection Laws were being put in place here in Spain and at last, there was hope for many ill-treated dogs.

How quickly a bubble can burst! It was dog walking day and we were all relaxing on the terrace. It had been a strenuous morning exercising 80+ dogs. We had just completed the adoption of Dasha, the last of our "Winter Puppies" and it was a happy day. It was then that the gate bell rang.

The reality of dog rescue is not all fluffy puppies and "happy ever afters", but we at Paradise do our best to shield our followers from the nasty stuff. This day shocked us and those of us that were there will never forget it.

A car towing an open trailer was parked outside and teetering precariously on it were three of the most stunning dogs. They were secured by their necks with wire and twine and were clearly terrified. We dare not think of what their history was – we just had to get them to the safety of our kennels. As we took each one from the truck you could sense their fear slip away. Big *Tony* the Male Mastin had clearly never been lead walked before and it took three of us to encourage him into a pen. Next was beautiful *Kira* a silver Shepherd mix, so loving and friendly, a nursing mother, her five puppies shut in the boot of the car.

Lastly and saddest for us was a big Mastin girl, also producing milk, but where were her puppies? We were told her name was *Purina* but that was the extent of the information given. The man that brought them was one of our regular blackmailers:

If you don't take them, I will take them far into the mountains and …

We all sigh because he knows we will. We led Purina into the large exercise area and the sight of her sad face was haunting. Do dogs cry? I think so.

The puppies were named – Paco, Panda, Portia, Poppy and Pedro – and quickly settled into the Puppy House. Four looking very much like little German Shepherds and one little pure white odd fellow with a black patch on his eye. It's very easy to be wise after the event, but was this one the puppy of Purina? He had such a Mastin look about him. Had Purina been cast out for not producing enough puppies? We'll never know and the total shock of this unexpected arrival didn't let us think straight. With hindsight, we should have given her the puppy to nurse but we just wanted to find her a place where she would feel safe and loved.

Our main tool for rehoming dogs is our Facebook page so we set to work to find a foster home for Purina. A horrible name, that sounded more like a dog food brand or a medical condition. We had to change it so I named her *Blossom* and started my campaign.

It only took a couple of days to find Blossom somewhere and we set off on the long drive to Almeria where she would be fostered in the hills above Albox. I was happy with this solution and once I was back home, I set to with finding homes for all the other new arrivals.

Unfortunately, in Rescue, there's always a curved ball to knock you off balance and for us it was a message to say that Blossom had escaped from her foster home and had been missing for two days. I can't explain the sick feeling I experienced. She was so far away from us but I knew I simply had to find her. For a week, I stayed up, day and night. I joined every Facebook group in Almeria that I could find and shared her information. The power of social media is extraordinary and very quickly we had over 1,000 shares.

She was spotted, captured and escaped again quite a distance from where we expected her to be. It was worrying as she was rapidly nearing the Autovia. The shares continued and after eight days a message came through that simply said, "I've got your dog". It was an unbelievable feeling of total relief and happiness. I set off at 4am the next morning on the long journey to collect her. I didn't take her back to the fosterers – instead we went straight back to Paradise.

We would never let Blossom go again and that was a promise. I made that promise every week at the kennels when I went for a cuddle. She was happy in our large dog area with her best friend and doppelgänger Marla, but Marla was about to be adopted which meant it was time to make my move. There was only one place for Blossom and that was with Alan and my two boys, Gordo and Jefe, the Samoyds.

I absolutely love her …
Blossiechops has come home!

Tied by the neck on a car trailer

Kira

Adopted by
LINDA WILSON

Kira

Introduction by MARY-ANN DUNNING

The pitiful sight of a stunning dog like Kira, tied with a wire round her neck and perched with two other dogs on a car trailer is heart wrenching. A new mum, her litter of puppies shut in the car boot. It is sad to say that as horrible as it was, this was preferable to the unthinkable alternative. Her story tugged at Linda Wilson's heart strings too, but in a good way. As soon as her puppies were weaned, Kira was on her way to Scotland.

Kira's story by Linda Wilson

Kira now lives in Scotland, which is a bit cooler than sunny Spain but she's acclimatising. She stays with Derek and I but there are always plenty of other people in our house. Twin granddaughters (aged 7) and now a newborn grandson who she is besotted with. She has to lie beside him and gets quite worried if he cries.

Kira loves to come down to the school with us and gets surrounded by children – she laps up all the attention. We also have three cats, who she is great with. She is still a bit 'iffy' with other cats, including Rupert across the road who used to be a regular visitor. He doesn't trust her - wise boy!

Kira has been a great girl and settled down really well. The day after she arrived, she was at the twins sixth birthday party with their other grandparents, my daughter's Labrador and two cats and never bothered at all. Her only problem (quite natural for the breed) is separation anxiety but that is getting better all the time.

We had a bit of a toileting problem at first but not too bad and only to be expected. Kira likes to chase rabbits and squirrels and then has VERY selective hearing and tunnel vision. So far, she has brought us three rabbits and a squirrel, all dead sorry to say. Kira is our third rescue and to anyone thinking of it I would say … go ahead it's so worthwhile but just have patience and understanding and you'll be so rewarded.

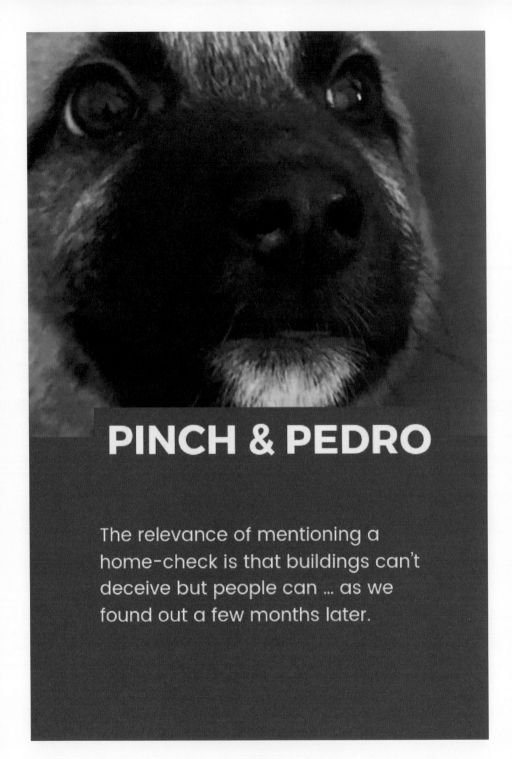

PINCH & PEDRO

The relevance of mentioning a home-check is that buildings can't deceive but people can ... as we found out a few months later.

Pinch and Pedro

Story by MARY-ANN DUNNING

Having survived being locked in a car boot while their mum (Kira) perched on the trailer, Pinch, Pedro and their other litter-mates soon settled in to the Paradise Puppy House.

As soon as details of the 'P' puppies were posted on Facebook, they started to attract attention. Pinch was full of life and was soon adopted and went off to her new home in the north east of England. Pedro was a different matter; for a time, we were doubtful that he would make it. Lots of love and careful attention helped to build him up and he gradually began to thrive. Pedro finally attracted the attention of someone in Torrevieja and, with a satisfactory home-check completed, he moved in with his new owner. The relevance of mentioning a home-check is that buildings can't deceive but people can … as we found out a few months later.

It transpired that Pedro's new owner had gone back to Finland but had not taken him with him – Pedro had simply been abandoned and left locked in the house! With the help of a neighbour, we managed to get him released and transported back to the kennels but, by this time, the beautiful boy was skin and bones. His claws were long and curled under and it was obvious that he had been totally neglected. Once again, we were faced with the challenge of building him up … but this time for a happier outcome.

Pedro now lives with his sister, Pinch, and has joined her family with Danny Allon, a climbing instructor in the UK. The two siblings have been reunited and are living a wonderful outdoor life full of love, fun and adventure.

Left to die by the side of the road

Ghost

Adopted by
DENNIS
POLKINGHORNE

Ghost

Introduction by MARY-ANN DUNNING

Colleen's husband, Peter, was driving along one of the mountain roads above La Murada when he spotted a 'dead' dog lying in the road. He pulled up to try to move the dog away from the traffic when the dog's tail gave a tiny flicker.

There was only one thing for it … into the back of the truck, home to Paradise for rehabilitation and rehoming with Dennis who totally adores him.

Ghost's story by Dennis Polkinghorne

Ghost is the best dog I have ever had. He is so obedient, loves other animals and adores children. My next door neighbour has a little boy and Ghost loves to say hello by giving him a lick every morning – they are best friends.

I spend more money on Ghost than I do on myself – bones, toys, and I even had to buy an estate car for him to go to the beach and play with the other dogs!

Ghost likes to make himself comfortable. At night we fight for the bed but he normally wins! He loves to lie with his front paws crossed and have his back rubbed.

Last week, Ghost had his first professional grooming. He was such a good dog for the lady and is so handsome!

> "
I think dogs are the most amazing creatures; they give unconditional love. For me, they are the role model for being alive.

- GILDA RADNER

LITTLE BILLY

I will never ever stop being grateful that you brought Billy into my life, I know I can speak on behalf of my family too. He's adored, loved and kissed every single day.

ADOPTED BY JULIA BETTS

Little Billy

Introduction by MARY-ANN DUNNING

It was a race against time for three little puppies and two little dogs being held in Huesca Killing Station.

Word was going round about them … they had four days to be rescued and talk of it was moving swiftly round the different rescue organisations.

One of our indoor pens just happened to be free so Colleen offered it for these little dogs. After a Facebook appeal to fund their release and transport, a generous rescue group called Pheonix in the UK stepped in and funded the whole process. Pretty quickly, beating the kill deadline by hours, the little group of puppies arrived at Paradise in the back of a van.

We were told that the three siblings were French Bulldog crosses and that became very apparent as their ears grew and grew and grew! Two little sandy coloured ones were homed locally but Little Billy a dear little black boy was about to start his big adventure … he was off to England.

Billy's story by JULIA BETTS

At the time Billy came to my attention on Facebook I was grieving for my dog Sadie, a beautiful German Shepherd/Border Collie cross who had passed away in March. I wasn't sure I would ever get another dog at that time, actually I was quite strongly opposed to the idea, but my family were worried about my mental health because being without the company of a dog was affecting me badly.

Then Billy's little face popped up on Facebook. I discussed it with my family and decided to go ahead and apply to adopt him. The adoption process was good and obviously went ahead as Billy was brought to me on the 6th of July 2018. He was scared and timid when he arrived so we sat outside in the garden with him most of the time and just chatted and kept an eye on him and let him find his own way. It takes time and cannot be rushed.

My rescue story is a very happy one, my experience with Paradise was and still is a very happy one. They are wonderful people who work so hard and are so dedicated. Once you have adopted a dog (or two) from Paradise you are part of the family. You can always contact them and ask for advice and they are always interested to know how your relationship is going with your dog.

I will never ever stop being grateful that you brought Billy into my life. I know I can speak on behalf of my family too. He's still learning, as am I, and we are still getting to know each other but things get better every day. He makes everybody laugh with his funny character. He's got loads of friends at the park and sometimes has his little friend Chester comes round for playtime in the garden. Billy loves to find a nice stick and carry it all the way home which makes me so proud.

I highly recommend adopting. I am enjoying every single second of watching my boy's confidence grow and seeing him happy. We send regular updates to Paradise and even included Billy's DNA results … after all, they really did need to know exactly how he inherited those ears!

50% French Bulldog

12.5% Parson Russell Terrier

37.5% Breed Groups (Terrier)

Bear

Adopted by
JANE RANKIN

Bear

Introduction by MARY-ANN DUNNING

Colleen went to the local council run dog pound to get a specific dog released. While she was there, she saw Bear shut in a cage on his own, in a terrible state and due to be killed the next morning. When she walked over to the cage, Bear put his paw through the mesh with a pitiful look. That was it … Colleen got him released there and then and took him home to Paradise!

Bear's story by Jane Rankin

Bear now lives in Pinar de Campoverde in Alicante with his forever family.

It was love at first sight but it took a long time for Bear to learn to trust us. He had been with us for about a year when we came in one day to be greeted by 65kg of furry muscle jumping up and down and making such a happy noise. It was that moment when we knew that he had accepted us and finally felt safe. We love him with all our hearts and he is now such a very big part of our family.

Abandoned as a tiny puppy

Princess Leia

Adopted by the
NALBORCZYK
FAMILY

Princess Leia

Introduction by MARY-ANN DUNNING

Another ring on the gate bell … this time Colleen was greeted by a local farmer dragging a cowering female Galgo on a rope. That was bad enough until he produced two tiny puppies – one from each coat pocket – and thrust them into Colleen's arms. They still had their eyes closed and could only be a matter of days old.

Princess Leia's story by Moira Nalborczyk

Princess Leia lives with Daddy Alex, Mummy Moira, human brother Elliot, dog brother Mac, dog sister Trixie and cat sister Ruby. After getting into conversation with Mary-Ann, on the terrace of a local cafe, I told her about wanting a Galgo puppy. She explained how a Galgo called Mama Mia had recently been rescued by Paradise, along with two of her puppies – a black one and a white one – and how all three now needed homes. Being lovers of black dogs, we expressed our interest and had our first meeting with our baby soon after this encounter. It was love at first sight. With her new name Princess Leia, she fitted straight in with the family.

At 12 weeks she was a rather large puppy who loved sunbathing even though she is mostly black. She spends ages chasing flies, pieces of fluff, fallen leaves and petals and adores her toys (we have gone through many toys). She has her manic sessions racing round the garden and these usually end up with a dramatic collapse and her sleeping to recharge her batteries. In fact, her curly tail only stops spinning when she sleeps.

Princess Leia has razor sharp teeth that can cut into anything she chooses to destroy and clearly has a very keen eye for interior design – this is a talent all puppy parents will understand. Her eyes speak volumes and she has fine-tuned the sympathy stare when flashing the whites with her head dipped. She is cute, boisterous, very loud and cheeky. She regularly voices her opinion, whether it be a high pitched whine or a deep bark, and her yawns are adorable as they are a very high pitched squeak.

When Princess Leia wants to play, we have no option but to drop what we are doing and oblige. Her brother Mac (a rescue greyhound) is her rock. If he is in the room she is calm. However, he finds her extended kissing sessions a bit exhausting so often retires to a bedroom! She loves playing with her sister Trixie who is our other Spanish rescue dog. Being her senior, Trixie tries to keep Princess Leia in check. Princess Leia has completed our fur family. We adore her and feel blessed having her in our lives.

> The bond with a
> true dog is as lasting
> as the ties of this
> earth will ever be.

- KONRAD LORENZ

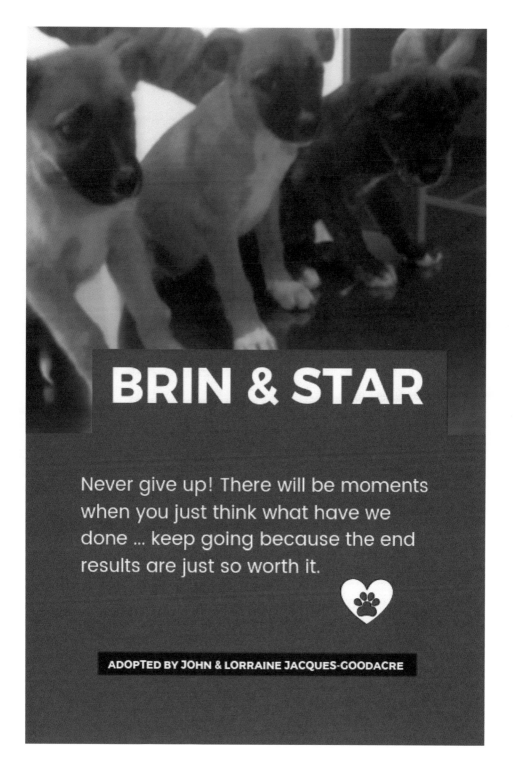

BRIN & STAR

Never give up! There will be moments when you just think what have we done ... keep going because the end results are just so worth it.

ADOPTED BY JOHN & LORRAINE JACQUES-GOODACRE

B rin & S tar

Story by LORRAINE JAQUES-GOODACRE

In January 2016, I saw on Facebook a photo of three puppies that were being kept in a cave at Hacienda Golf Resort near Sucina. Two guys living there were asking for help with funding for the puppies to have their first injections.

My husband (John) and I replied and that was the start of our beautiful story of owning two rescue dogs and getting to know the wonderful Colleen and Paradise Rescue Kennels.

We helped with the injections and some of my friends helped with donations too. The puppies were all very frightened. We learned that eight puppies had been born in a cave in the workers' compound at Hacienda Riquelme. It would seem that no local rescue was able to take the Mother and all the puppies but the guys had managed to successfully rescue three puppies who went to live temporarily in Murcia. Unfortunately, they had to stay in a dark underground garage during the day, which was not ideal, so ... International Team John and Lorraine to the rescue!

We decided to have them for a short time each day to socialise them. That lasted for two days when we decided they could not go back to that garage so we asked if we could have them permanently.

We only have a small apartment, but we built a run on our terrace. The first night, the three puppies who we had called Star, Brindle and Bruno were so scared – they pulled the cover off our BBQ and slept under it. The second night they were all howling at 2 o'clock in the morning. We had no idea why – we had never dealt with puppies before – they were hungry bless them, and once they had eaten they settled down.

We had a very big problem … in seven days time we had to return to the UK for two weeks and we could not find anyone to help locally with the puppies. We were in a state of panic! Eventually, after much asking around, we were told about Paradise Rescue Kennels. I called Colleen and she was totally amazing saying "*of course*" she would take them.

We met Colleen and saw the kennels. The three babies, Brindle, Star and Bruno were left with her to try to find them homes because we thought we could not have dogs because of our lifestyle, travelling, etc.

We went back to the UK and three weeks later contacted Colleen as we wanted to help with the socialisation of the puppies. When we returned Bruno had been rehomed to a Dutch couple in a motorhome who travel around Europe. They had previously had a dog from Colleen and this dog was very confident, so they chose Bruno because he was the most nervous and they felt their other dog could help him.

We kept visiting Brindle (now shortened to Brin) and Star and took them out in the orange groves on and off lead. They were so good and every time we visited they would peek over the wall to see us. They always touched our heart and we loved walking these growing bundles of fun but they were getting very attached to us. Colleen said that this was a potential problem as no-one else had shown any interest in them.

The day we decided to tell Colleen that we had fallen in love with the puppies, we said … if they show us a sign, we will have them. Off we trotted to the kennels and, sure enough from the entrance gate they knew we were there. Their heads popped up over the first wall as we walked down to the compound and along to the open puppy area. They ran through and Star climbed – yes climbed – the fencing and threw herself into John's arms, with one each of her front legs wrapped around his neck. Brin was still on the floor inside the puppy compound whimpering, he could not climb! So, Colleen climbed in and lifted him over the fence. We all said laughing *"there's the sign"* and the rest is history.

Brin and Star were transported over to the UK. At first, they were very nervous of people, particularly Brin. He did not like men and to this day they both hate cats. We are so lucky to have wonderful open fields and a river near where we live in Edenbridge, Kent. They love to run and play, and they enjoy playing in the river – not so the sea. They also love other dogs, lots of cuddles and treats.

Adopting two puppies has been hard work – there is no doubt about that – but now they have turned into wonderful loving dogs. They go training and have their Bronze Kennel Club awards, they have also been to agility too. They love travelling in the car and come to Spain with us on holiday but they now have their forever home!

My tip to anyone thinking of adopting a rescue dog is never give up! There will be moments when you just think what have we done … keep going because the end results are just so worth it.

Lost and alone in the mountains

Rambo

Adopted by
LESLEY ELDER

Rambo

Introduction by MARY-ANN DUNNING

A couple found a single little puppy up in the mountains when they were out walking. They brought it down to the kennels and asked Colleen if she could take it. She was very concerned that it was a single puppy and asked them if they would retrace their steps and see if there were any more. There was no sign of any more puppies or a mother so how he got to be on his own up there remains a mystery.

He was such a tiny thing so we originally called him Midge but such a handsome chap had to end up being called Rambo!

Rambo's story by Lesley Elder

Rambo now lives with his forever family, which includes Mummy and Daddy and two grey rescue cats called Smurf and Sidi, near the doggy beach in Gran Alacant.

Rambo is a real little hero! He saved the life of Sidi when we previously lived on a farm in Los Montesinos. Sidi had tried to drink from the reservoir and had fallen in. He couldn't get out and we only realised he was in there because Rambo came to tell us and took us to where Sidi was. Sidi was exhausted and trembling when we pulled him out. He would have probably drowned if Rambo hadn't spotted him and come to get us!

Since that day, Rambo has taken on an important role in our family – he is in charge of security! He does an excellent job and only barks when there is a 'threat'. He may be small but he barks like a big dog and takes his job very seriously.

We have learned to listen to Rambo's body language and different noises to understand him. Even though he can't talk, he is still communicating. Rambo taps you on the arm when he is hungry or needs a drink. He whimpers at the door for pee/poo time, and he has different barks for strangers and for strange cats or dogs.

One hint or tip for anyone thinking of rescuing a dog is that they need time to learn and settle in. There is a lot to learn at a new home. They need time to understand what you want them to do and to get into your routine.

Abandoned as a puppy

Athena

Adopted by
KARIN FALK

Athena

Introduction by MARY-ANN DUNNING

Young Maria Bettis, daughter of a fellow dog rescuer in Fortuna, heard that the owner of a litter of Boxer cross puppies couldn't find homes for them, and was taking them to the pound. Maria contacted Colleen to see if she could take them and personally raised the money to have them released and vaccinated.

Karin Falk is another of our loyal supporters and follows our Facebook page. As soon as we posted details of the new arrivals, she fell in love with one of the little puppies (originally named Primrose). We were delighted when Karin drove all the way from Sweden to collect her! It was an uneventful journey until her very large camper van broke down on our access road. Eventually it was repaired and after showering us with gifts of food, medicines, biscuits and toys, she was on her way with newly named Athena.

Athena's story by Karin Falk

Athena now lives with us and our other two dogs, Nick and Red, in a beautiful part of Sweden. She enjoys walks through the stunning scenery up in the mountains and loves the snow. She is a big strong girl living the best life we can give her.

Wherever I go, Athena is always by my side – a wonderful faithful friend.

We keep in touch with everyone at Paradise and it is such a shame that Athena's three sisters are still with them – they are a lovely trio.

66

Before you get a dog, you can't quite imagine what living with one might be like; afterward, you can't imagine living any other way.

- CAROLINE KNAPP

Foster family missed the bus!

Willow

Adopted by
SOPHIE
HOLLIDAY

W illow

Introduction by MARY-ANN DUNNING

Some of the Spanish Rescue Organisations are run very successfully from out of the country and by using foster homes. There exists a network of very reliable people, thoroughly screened who contribute to the smooth passage from rescue, through transport, to eventual arrival at the dog's new home. However, once in a while, as in Willow's case, a foster can fail and the well-oiled cogs can grind to a halt.

After agreeing to arrange for such things as immunisations, sterilisation and preparation for travel, poor Willow 'missed the bus' when her fosterer failed to meet the deadlines. When asked by the Rescue if Paradise could foster her for a couple of months, ensuring that everything was in place for her new travel date, we didn't hesitate and made the journey to Almeria. She was a lovely happy addition to the Paradise family and was everyone's favourite until she was spotted by Sophie and set off for her new life in the UK.

Willow's story by Sophie Holliday

Willow lives with me, Sophie, and my partner Cal in Tenbury Wells, Worcestershire. Cal's family are currently renovating a barn, so Willow spends all day there running around the fields with her brothers – our other two dogs, Ronnie and Pig. She has also become best friends with the family cat, Eric, and loves a cuddle!

Willow has a heart of gold and we love her so much. She spends every night in bed with us and will take a nap at every available moment.

Wherever there is water, she will find it and get in it without fail. She LOVES food. We can't take her anywhere without hearing 'look at those ears!'. Most of all, she is the cheekiest, happiest little dog with a heart of gold and we simply couldn't imagine life without her.

One thing she has taught us is to enjoy every day to the fullest. To anyone thinking of rescuing: Go for it!

We had never met Willow before we decided to adopt her and lots of people thought we were mad. But giving this little dog a chance was the best thing we have ever done and from the moment we saw that first photo we knew she was the one for us.

A cheeky Spanish stray

Chibs

Adopted by

BEX STEWART

Chibs

Introduction by Mary-Ann Dunning

Peter was heading back to the kennels in his truck when he caught a glimpse of movement. He and Colleen are always aware of their surroundings when out and about and their well-trained eyes have spotted many stray dogs over the years.

On this occasion, Peter realised there was a small dog running loose but was unable to catch it. He was struggling on crutches and, unfortunately, his attempts to clamber through the rocks were severely hampered. The little dog was always one step ahead and was not making things easy.

Peter visited the same spot again and again but still had no joy in finding the little stray. However, a couple of days later, good news arrived in the arms of a young boy Stevie who lived nearby. He had managed to catch the stray and brought him in to Paradise. It soon became obvious that he was a cheeky little heart melter and there was no doubt someone would fall in love with him very soon.

Chibs' story by Bex Stewart

After losing our previous dog Luna in May 2018, we weren't really looking to adopt another dog anytime soon but like many other people, I'm part of several adoption/rescue pages on Facebook and it was here I came across Paradise Kennels.

Mary-Ann had posted a photo of a little dog called 'Stevie' who was apparently named after the young boy who caught him as a stray. It was here that I first saw (and fell in love with) his adorable face. I went back and forth about whether we were ready to adopt another dog and told myself it was too soon. However, his little face kept popping up and I just knew it was meant to be. After I expressed an interest in Stevie, Mary-Ann and I exchanged several messages and the rest is, as they say, history.

I had reservations about adopting another Spanish dog because Luna had died from renal failure caused by undetected Leishmaniasis. I asked Mary-Ann to do a blood test before we committed to having him and fortunately this came back negative, I know that 'Leish' can lie dormant but it still gave us some peace of mind in the first instance.

On July 26th 2018, we drove to Bristol and met the guys who had driven Stevie all the way from Spain, then together we drove home to Cornwall.

Stevie is now called Chibs, named after my favourite character from Sons of Anarchy. He certainly made himself at home quite quickly and he loves nothing more than affection and cuddles. He's made friends with our youngest cat but unfortunately the older two don't like him quite so much! We keep them all separate to maintain peace in the house and it works for everyone.

Chibs loves playing with his many toys, running up the clay trails with my partner, playing with other dogs and exploring the woods, particularly so he can chase squirrels!

We have had to work hard to train Chibs. He is a strong willed dog who likes to try and dominate but he's come a long way and our perseverance is paying off.

Chibs is a great dog and I've lost count of how many times people have stopped us to tell us how handsome and unique he is. The best thing we ever did was adopt another dog and I'm happy that it was Chibs from Paradise.

PODENCO LOVE

Written through the eyes of
Jerry the Podenco about his life with
Heather & Richard Price

I'm Jerry 'Mr Brown Nose', a spotty Podenco boy
I'm going to tell my story and share my lifetime joy
I'll try to describe the magic, from puppy days 'til old
I know that I was ugly, but my character had you sold
I don't recall my kennel name, for I wasn't at Paradise long
I was so very lucky that my new mum came along
I wasn't cute and fluffy, but you took me home to see
If I settled in ok with you, a family life for me
My skinny legs and pointy ears, no tail just a stub
Unable to wag, it wiggled instead, when my tummy got a rub.

You used to call me *Jezzer*, a name I didn't mind
I was just so grateful that this home was warm and kind
When dad was out you sang to me, less a song but more this
sound
Yummy Yummy Yummy I've got love in my tummy, I feel it going
round and round!
Dog discos and dancing, or counting my spots with tunes
Thank God no one saw you, you'd be locked up with the loons!

Our love it grew so quickly, at times I couldn't hide
How happy I was to be with you and guard our home with pride
I never did things slowly, I used to bang and bash
And scrape your fresh new paintwork, clumsy with a crash
I'm sorry for the damage, I've left behind my mark
Footprints in the concrete, the memory of my bark
Then, over excited once, I slipped into the pool
Dad jumped in to save me, my lifeguard acted cool
The panic it was over, not bearing any harms
I felt a little soggy, but safer in your arms.

Your friends and clients loved me, summer time was merry
They often gave me silly names, but my favourite was *Just Jerry*
They said they came for sunshine and wanted time with you
The truth behind their visits, was seeing Jerry too
I let them feed me titbits and joined in holiday games
They sent me gifts for Christmas, regardless of my names

I looked forward to my birthday, great parties you did make
Prezzies, treats and paper hats, with candles on my cake.

Our special time was winter, Dad and me on the rug
Frolic games and playtime, ending with a hug
Dog hair mess gave Mum the stress, "hoover it" she cried
It's ok, there is no mess, Dad he always lied
Stealing from your garden, apricots, olives and lime
Sorry Mum I've made more mess, but had a really good time
You always were so patient, I rarely made you cross
If Dad and me remembered, at home our Mum's the boss
From my doggy heart I thank you, I hope I let it show
This Paradise boy who came to stay, and the love I learned to
know.

Christmas time with just us three, a pile of presents under the tree
Treats and toys I longed to see, kind old Santa left loads for me
My turkey roast and gravy, plus Sprouts the bestest part
Then I was in trouble, cos Brussels made me fart!
I wasn't permitted on the sofa , the rule was more a guide
A lapse idea I tried to keep, but never could abide
Famous once I made it to print, a calendar boy back page
Dad too scared to pose for a month, he said it would show his
age.

As I got old and slow, you said I needed a friend
My peaceful campo lifestyle, swiftly came to an end
Off you went to Paradise, I waited with baited breath
In came *Ruby* puppy sister, who stayed with me 'til death
I hope I taught her well, still young and not too clever
"Trust in them" I told her, they'll love you now forever
It's not just us you rescued, before was Captain Jack
My fluffy naughty brother, except his nose was black
I cared for him in old age, as Ruby did for me
But I am known as favourite, from my story you can see.

As you finally wed, woofs of joy I shed, when my parents said "I Do"
I couldn't be there, to watch and share, but my heart it was with you
I know in time you'll manage, without my lazy days
Replaced by youngster Ruby, and all her crazy ways
I cherish the magic most, of how our family rocked
Never angry or mad at four legged friends, our place in your hearts was locked.

As I got poorly, you never gave up
Trying to heal with help from the pup
Then when my time it came, to say goodbye and part
I know it made you sad as I slept and broke your heart
I counted myself lucky, so please keep hold of this
My magical life with you two, memories sealed with a kiss.

From day one I loved you, adored you with my paws
Nothing could divide us, I was forever yours
The time we had together will last forever, yet while
You talk of me and reminisce, fond things to make you smile
As you miss my bark, woofs and licks, don't worry I'm looking your way
From puppy heaven with furry friends, I see you everyday.

Podenco Love
Jerry Price (2008-2019)

66

Everybody should have a shelter dog. It's good for the soul.

- PAUL SHAFFER

Adoption
hints and tips

Adopting a dog

Important information – Dr Lesley Hunter

Adopting a dog is not a decision to be taken lightly. Although Paradise often has puppies to rehome, many dogs from rescue centres in Spain have a chequered past that often includes abuse and/or previous failed adoptions.

> Just being a dog lover is not enough …
> you need to be a dog lover with a big
> heart and plenty of patience!

There is nothing more frustrating and distressing than someone who adopts a dog – builds up expectations of a happy life and forever home – then returns the dog the minute the going gets tough. All dogs are hard work! Rescue dogs can undoubtedly bring additional challenges, but perseverance and patience will work wonders.

Dogs are highly adaptable creatures. They don't care what nationality you are and will often thrive in homes and environments very different from their origin. The barriers created by fear of breed characteristics, travel regulations and medical conditions are reflections from the human owners and not from the dogs themselves. So, here is some basic information to dispel some of the myths and help to put some of the previous stories and case studies from Paradise into context.

Preparation for adoption

Any respectable rescue centre will require potential adopters to provide detailed information about their living environment and should, where possible, follow up with a home-check visit.

Here are some typical questions and points to consider:

- How would you describe your household and living environment?
- What are the occupations of the household members?
- What are the working hours of the household members?
- Is your property owned or rented?
- If rented, do you have permission from the owner/landlord to have a dog in the property?
- Is there sufficient (appropriate) indoor space for a dog?
- Is there sufficient (appropriate) outdoor space for a dog?
- Are all indoor and outdoor areas adequately secure for a dog?
- Where will the dog sleep?
- Where will the dog be when left alone?
- How often will the dog be left alone, and for how long?
- Who will be the primary carer for the dog?
- How physically active is this person?
- What experience does this individual have with (a) dogs, (b) rescue dogs, and (c) this particular breed of dog?

- Where (and how often) will the dog be walked?
- Where (and how often) will the dog have access to food and water?
- Will the dog be in a home with other animals? If so – what and how many? What are the temperaments of these other animals?
- Will the dog be in a home with children? If so – how many and what ages? What experiences have these children had around dogs?
- Where will the dog be if/when you go on holiday?
- Do you intend to insure the dog? Who with?
- Which vet will you register the dog with?
- Are there any circumstances that would cause you to return a dog to rescue? If so – what?

Transport and travel

Many dogs that are adopted in Spain remain in Spain. Paradise has many dogs still living in local areas but many of their ex-residents have travelled far and wide to other countries including the UK, Norway, Sweden, Finland, France, Holland, Belgium, Luxembourg and Portugal.

Travel with dogs is relatively easy but it is essential to check the relevant requirements and regulations in advance.

In 2001, the movement of animals was made easier between mainland Europe and the UK with the introduction of the Pet Travel Scheme. There were still strict rules to adhere to but the mandatory six month quarantine ceased to exist. A number of reliable pet transport companies became established with Defra approved, air conditioned vans. All had to comply with the UK Government's rules and it became a relatively straightforward procedure to be able to send dogs out of Spain for adoption. At the time of writing, the future is less certain regarding pet travel to and from the UK. It is a worrying time for all rescue kennels and the recommendation is that anyone wishing to adopt in Spain and wanting to travel with their dog(s) should always check the latest advice from the UK Government website.

https://www.gov.uk/guidance/pet-travel-to-europe-after-brexit

Advisory information for Spain

Information provided by CENTRO VETERINARIO BENICAN for advice only

Parasite borne diseases

Many areas of Spain have a climate that is perfect for supporting the lifecycles of ticks, mosquitoes and sand-flies, all of which can transmit potentially lethal diseases to dogs.

Ticks transmit diseases such as Ehrlichia and Rickettsia (both prevalent in the area local to Paradise Rescue Kennels), Lyme Disease and Anaplasma (more prevalent in the north of Spain, but not unheard of locally). Mosquitos transmit Dirofilaria (also known as Heartworm) and Sand-flies transmit Leishmania.

All these diseases can be potentially fatal to dogs, but most can be cured. Unfortunately, although Leishmania can be controlled it is the one disease that cannot be cured. Hence why it is the most well-known. It is therefore important to understand the potential signs and symptoms of these diseases, to allow early treatment, but it is also fundamental to take precautions to protect your animals.

Protection against parasite borne diseases

External protection with pipettes and collars is simple and there are annual vaccinations against both Heartworm and Leishmania. There are also alternative preventive medicines available in oral form for both diseases for people who prefer not to vaccinate their dogs.

It is important to make clear that Leishmania is not a death sentence as it retains this stigma and people are sometimes terrified of dogs with it, making it harder to find them adoptions. Whilst it is a life-long disease which requires blood tests and treatment, it is perfectly manageable, and many dogs lead a normal life.

Rabies vaccination

Rabies vaccinations are mandatory and must be updated annually in Spain as opposed to the UK where the vaccination is valid for three years. This is a point of confusion for many people, particularly when travelling between Spain and the UK with their pets.

Microchipping and registration

It is always advised to have your dog microchipped. However, unlike in other countries, Spain does not have a national microchip database, rather relying on regional databases. This can cause a problem if you adopt a dog in one region then move to live in another region without re-registering the microchip.

What happens if your dog goes missing? Vets can only access an owner's details in the microchip database of the region in which they work. So, if your dog is found and they are registered in a different region to where you live (or where the vet that reads the microchip is based) they will not be able to access your details to get your dog back to you!

It is therefore really important to make sure that your dog is registered with the relevant authorities in the appropriate region and that all of your details are kept up-to-date. This is usually done by visiting the local Ayuntamiento (Town Hall) with all the relevant documentation for your dog.

Registration needs to happen regardless of whether or not your animal already has a microchip from your home country or is getting a new Spanish microchip.

Dangerous dog breeds

Under Spanish Law, some dogs will fall under the category 'Potentially Dangerous Dog Breed' and will require a more detailed registration process. It is best to take advice from a local veterinary clinic to ensure you identify if this applies to your dog and to follow the correct procedures for the specific region of Spain.

Spanish dog breeds

Galgos and Podencos are by far the most frequently abandoned dogs in this part of Spain and unfortunately this will most likely continue to be the case for many years to come.

Both breeds are popular for hunting and once they have reached the end of their 'useful life' in the eyes of the hunter they are often abandoned rather than rehomed. This normally happens to the dogs at a young age as something as simple as a limp can be enough for the hunters to abandon the dogs. Many times, they are found abandoned with fractured legs, making their care in rescue centres all the more complicated due to the expensive surgery and aftercare these kinds of injuries require. They are also frequently abused, and vets often see horrendous scarring all over their body as they have little fur and thin skin meaning they are very visible.

Many charities have been set us exclusively to rescue these breeds of dogs, but the scale of the problem is such that they are often well over-capacity due to the sheer number of dogs being abandoned. Despite this, both Galgos and Podencos can make excellent pets.

A conversation with
COLLEEN

What or whom has been your greatest influence?

My heart is full because of my love for my animals. I know where it came from, it came from my father, he was the same, he loved all animals.

I was five years old when we came from Ireland, to live in Doncaster, Yorkshire. We never had a lot of money when I was a child, but my dad always said that if you had food in your belly and a roof over your head, then you had enough.

My dad got me my first dog, Smokey Joe, a black Greyhound. We loved him, unlike my mother as Smokey was a devil. He bit the postman, the dustbin men, anyone he didn't want on our property. He was a terrible thief, stealing whatever he could, but we still loved him. He lived till he was 18 years old and I never got over losing him.

People used to call at our house with sick animals and dad would make them well again. People didn't have the money for vets back then. I looked up to my dad as I watched him help all who came to him.

So, this is where I get my love for animals from. It has grown more and more in my lifetime. From our Donkey Sanctuary in Ireland to my home now in Spain with all my beloved animals. I cannot see myself doing anything else. My heart is full, my work goes on till I die. I love my animals. Simple as that.

Have you always worked with animals or did you and Peter do other things?

No. Before I met Peter, I was in the British Army Medical Corps and Peter was a Graphic Designer and a drummer in a band. He's played with some well-known groups in his time. He later became a builder. Peter built Paradise Kennels.

Before moving here to Spain, where did you live?

I was born in Ireland but as a family, when I was still a child, we moved to Doncaster in Yorkshire. Peter and I moved to Ireland later and brought up our children, Kerry and Steve over there.

When did you first get involved with rescuing animals on the larger scale?

We were driving near our property in Ireland when we picked up two neglected donkeys, walking along the road. They were skin and bones. We lived in 10 acres and so we took them home and looked after them. Peter built a 60-foot stable block and that was the start of the Dysart Donkey Sanctuary. We had 80 donkeys, two pigs, numerous dogs, cats, birds, geese and a Jersey Cow.

How did you end up coming to Spain to live?

We retired … that was the intention! We decided on Spain as my health wasn't good and my arthritis and Crohn's Disease seemed better in the warm. We came over with a big Irish Wolf Hound and I actually paid to buy a big Mastin. I didn't realise back then about the situation with stray dogs.

How did your retirement become a 24/7 labour of love?

Because I lived here for a couple of years on my own, so I didn't get bored, Peter built me a few runs to board dogs. I had no thoughts of running a Rescue Kennels but when we found a Podenco that we called Roxy, then six Galgo puppies under a slab, we decided that I would board in half the runs and that could fund stray dogs in the other half.

Has any one dog touched you more than the hundreds of others that you've rescued?

Tango, my big ginger and white Podenco. He was found up in the mountains near Hendon and suffered from Epilepsy. I spent many, many hours, soothing him after one of his many seizures. He died quite recently at seven years of age, doing what he loved best – guarding the kennels from the roof of the Puppy House.

If you won the Lottery, what would you do with your winnings?

Firstly, I would take care of my family – my two children and five grandchildren.

Of course, it would depend on how much I won, but my dream would be to buy a bigger place, here in Spain but keeping Paradise as well. I would need lots of land for my ideas.

I would like a "Commune" for dogs. They would all have their own houses built and dog loving families to live with them. I would take all old dogs handed in to killing stations. The houses would belong to the dogs for however long they have left. I would choose the families who would live with them and look after them. I would have huge play areas with pools for them to play in during the summer. Lots of shade. Lovely quiet areas for scared dogs. This is my dream. It would take a lot of money, but even a million Euros would make a lot of difference to a lot of dogs.

References and useful links

1. Spain tops euro table for abandoned pets.
   https://www.thelocal.es/20140618/spain-tops-euro-table-for-abandoned-pets

2. Worrying statistics for abandoned animals in Spain.
   https://www.euroweeklynews.com/2019/07/02/worrying-statistics-for-abandoned-animals-in-spain/

3. "Él nunca lo haría" ("They'd never do it to you"): a study by Fundación Affinity into the abandonment and adoption of pets in Spain in 2018: https://www.fundacion-affinity.org/sites/default/files/whitepaper-abandono-2019-en.pdf

Paradise Website
http://paradiserescuekennels.com

Paradise has a strong presence on Facebook with three separate pages/groups.

   i. Paradise Rescue Kennels – general Facebook page with information and news about the kennels.

   ii. Purely Paradise Rehoming Page – specific page for current Paradise dogs looking for homes.

   iii. Paradise Rescue Kennels Donation Page – information page providing details of fundraising activities – you can access this page by searching for @ParadiseRescueKennelsBenferri on Facebook.

Sponsors

The following businesses have generously provided sponsorship to buy the initial batch of books for Paradise to sell and raise much needed funds.

PLATFORM1 bar and bistro

4YourPaws

Rådgivning i Spanien

Avalon Funeral Plans Spain

Veterinary information for Spain has been provided by
Centro Veterinario BENICAN

This book has been produced and published by
Dr. Lesley Hunter
Pack Leader Publications

PLATFORM1 bar and bistro

Located in Guardamar, this bar bistro endeavours to cater for everyone with a food menu to suit all tastes.

Carrer Ramon y Cajal, 21, 03140 Guardamar del Segura

Call 684 02 78 17 | Facebook @Platform1Bar

4YourPaws

A family run team of animal lovers headed by Elliot who is City and Guilds qualified and experienced in Animal Care. We offer dog walking, pet sitting and Vet visit pick up and drop off services.

Printed in Poland
by Amazon Fulfillment
Poland Sp. z o.o., Wrocław

50144658R00072